A MOSAIC
OF MEMORIES

THE INTERNATIONAL LIBRARY OF PHOTOGRAPHY

PICTURE.COM

Andrew Branch, Editor

A Mosaic Of Memories

Library of Congress
Cataloging in Publication Data

ISBN 0-7951-5319-8

Printed in China

Published by
The International Library of Photography
3600 Crondall Lane
Suite 101
Owings Mills, MD 21117

FOREWORD

Writing about photography is a difficult task, as it entails the translation of one art form into another. While every photograph may not inspire a thousand words, it is easy to see how the saying evolved. Words are a function of the intellect. But, much like music, a visual image speaks directly to the emotions, evoking an immediate and powerful response. Only when one attempts to analyze, interpret, and critique this image do words come into play.

As one views a photograph, one is slowly taken on a visual journey through the eye of the photographer. Whether the photograph was staged or the "point-and-click method" was employed, the picture represents the fact that moments in time pass within the blink of an eye. The photographer not only captures a scene or a subject; he also creates a lasting, tangible image of a fleeting instant. The beauty of photography is that any individual can produce an image of these passing moments.

Photography represents both an active and a passive art form. The degree to which a photographer participates in his art form varies from photograph to photograph. The photographer can either tell a story within the photograph, or simply stand aside and record life as it happens. The one thing that holds true for all photography is this: without the photographer there can be no photograph. Even in a simple snapshot, the photographer's influence is clearly evident.

The photographs within this anthology exhibit their own importance as well as demonstrate the importance of the photographer. In some cases, the idea or photo found the photographer. For instance, while taking pictures on a nature hike, a photographer may catch the sunset as it breaks through a bunch of trees, and thus an idea may be born. In other instances, a photographer may orchestrate and choreograph the set-up of a photograph in order to fulfill a creative idea or notion. (This may be the case in still-life or abstract photography.)

Another similar element in most of these photographs is the photographer's love of and dedication to his subject. For example, nature photography is often captured by devoted nature watchers. Those people who take humorous photographs usually enjoy the lighter side of life and tend to look for the funniest aspect of any situation. The numerous photographs of children in this book were most likely taken by parents or grandparents who appreciate the joy and wonderment contained in a child's smile. Becoming emotionally involved with a subject, through deep love or interest, often enables a photographer to generate ideas that help him capture the true essence of his subject.

There are also photographers who gain inspiration not from relating to one specific subject or another, but rather from focusing on the photographic process itself. They often use special techniques to create images they have envisioned within their own minds, or they choose to concentrate on one particular aspect of photography (such as lighting) and through experimentation examine its effect on a particular subject. By casting aside conventional approaches, these photographers open different pathways to new ideas, allowing their own imaginations to roam freely.

No matter how or why a photograph is taken, the viewer must realize that each photograph represents an individual's artistic viewpoint. There are many excellent photographs contained in this anthology. At a quick glance they might appear to be just pictures, but be sure to focus on the ideas being conveyed, both emotionally and physically. Allow yourself to become lost in the photo: perhaps you may gain a new understanding of it, or you may simply be able to relate more deeply to the photographer's viewpoint.

Andy Warhol once predicted that in the future everyone will have his fifteen minutes in the spotlight. This philosophy could easily be applied to photography by simply stating that every subject has its moment, and as a photographer, one must strive to find and capture these instants. After all, these cherished moments, which may seem frozen in time when we see them through the camera's viewfinder, do not last fifteen minutes; rather, viewing a photograph that captures these instances may trigger memories that will always remain embedded deep within our minds. Through photographs we are therefore offered a physical reminder as an accompaniment to a memory. We then hold in our hands the permanency of a cherished moment in time—an image of yesterday.

Russell Hall
Senior Editor

Elizabeth Ann Parton　　　　　　　　　People
Dreaming

Matthew Bradon Murphy　　　　　　　Children
Phillies Fan

Andy Anthony Alcaraz　　　　　　　Animals/Pets
Yummy

Chad Michael Raught　　　　　　　　Children
Easter Angel

James Bradley Laverty　　　　　　　Travel
Beauty In A Brazilian Slum

Marcia Kay Streitberger　　　　　　　Nature
Hummingbird

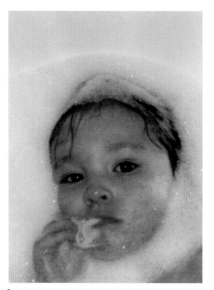

T. J. Gallagher   People
Bubbles Of Fun

Lauren Elizabeth Stein   Nature
God Revealing

Nicole L. Downey   Children
Kai

Chase Anthony Cabral   Nature
Ocean Walkway

Kiril Petrov   Children
Kristina

Heather Stockwell   Animals/Pets
Sharing A Sunset

Douglas A. Boudrow   Other
Facing The Red Devil

Kaitlin Danone Freeman   People
Once Upon A Time

Erin Rebecca Ward Young   People
Untitled

Richard L. Chu   Other
Abandoned Safe

Nick Hartstang   Nature
Camo-Frogged

Jonna Crutchfield   Children
My Angel—Thomas E. Johnson

Stacy Jeanne Gatling　　　　　　　Nature
Guarding The Nest

Brandon Michael Winns　　　　　　Nature
Hidden Wafers

Drew Taylor　　　　　　　　　　Nature
Serene Sunset

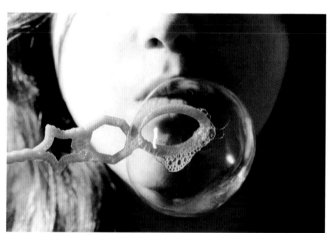

Yvette Kirkland　　　　　　　　Children
Blowing Bubbles

Robert R. Owen　　　　　　　　　Nature
Can You Hear It?

Cynthia P. Gurino　　　　　　Animals/Pets
Princess Zara Alexandra Gurino

Chelsey Rae Anderson   Children
Connar And Tanner

Sarah Easterly   Nature
Sunrise

Leo Lax   Nature
Regeneration

Janet L. Ackerman   Nature
Spring

Annette Brown   Children
Not Quite Big Enough

Brenda Granger   Travel
Lakeview

Mladen Beganovic   Animals/Pets
Captive

Theresa Lynn Schroder   Other
Colorado Sunset

Taylor Tedford   Other
Leaning Building

Margaret L. White   Animals/Pets
Grevy's Zebra Orphan

Kaitlyn E. Burnett   Nature
The Dragon's Tale

Josh Bentley Williamson   Action
Hope

Susan Gayle Armstrong   Animals/Pets
Guarded By An Angel

Kelly Schomaker   Children
Butterflies

Kelly Marie McCarty   Nature
A New Day

Alan Bennett Ilagan   Nature
The Sun From Behind

Traci Lynn Young   Animals/Pets
Missy

Tara Jane Raftovich   People
Milton

Dawn Angela McClelland   Animals/Pets
Pigeon Lunch

Corey Thomas White   Humor
Just Me

Evan Thomas Kramer   Travel
El Templo De Debod Y La Puesta Del Sol

Melissa A. Senick   People
Daddy's Little Girl

Nick Wisner   Nature
Untitled

Ross Sublett Haley   Travel
Evening

Chelsea Grace Burton   Nature
Frosted Bloom

Amy Renee Brookman   Portraiture
Beach Gaze

Louis James Gaeta   Nature
Buck Deer

Denise Evans Visintine   Travel
Capitola

Alex C. Druien   Nature
Summer Fun

Sara Pekar   Children
Tears Of The Sun

John Spencer Jenkins   People
Speak

Misty Ann Likens   Children
Thirsty Baby

Lloyd Stolworthy   Portraiture
In Honor Of Chet Atkins

Mary-Kate Laird   Other
Illuminating View

Pamela D. Brydie   Nature
Weathered

Wyatt Randall Queen   Nature
Bee Happy

Heather Phelps   Children
Very Curious!

Adam Michael Tyrrell   Nature
Rolling In

Traci R. Walther   Nature
Autumn Trees

David James Iliyn   Animals/Pets
Africa—Lion Cub

Seung Woo Kim   Travel
Hope

Janet Rose Hollenbach   Other
Final Sunset

Patrick Anthony Baker   Travel
Untitled

Thomas Watson Dutton   Children
Siblings And Friends

Jennifer Anne McIntosh   Nature
Walking In Winter Wind

Debbie Ann Mason   Children
Neal Jr.

Robert Joseph Phelps   People
Gimme A Kiss

Justin Todd Miller   Children
Brayden Wayne

Patrick William Conn   Nature
Up The Road

Hal Burris   Nature
Frog And Pumpkin

Amy Beth Corsetto   Nature
Velburg, Germany

Candy Thompson Paine   Children
Mo-Mo's Three Diamonds

Siengthong Vongphouthone   Travel
Love To Our Country

Fahrinisa Fatima Kevser Oswald   Nature
Cape Cod Low Tide

Margareth Lyra Prado   Children
Water Fairies

Adam Grant Chapman   Nature
Summer In Hungary

Meghan Grace Delozier   Portraiture
Hands

Natalia Popova   Nature
Frozen Mirror

Kristen Nicole Longnecker   Other
Engaged

Brad T. D. Skeldon   Nature
Sweet Sunset

Steve Jones Travel
Golden Buddha At Night

Barbara Thomas Nature
"Beeing" Floral

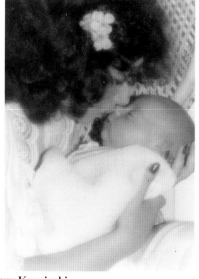

Charles Henry Karpinski Portraiture
Wife And Child

Josephine Wallace Nature
Az

Carrie L. LeClair Children
That Was Some Good Eating!

Clare Terry Dejacomo Travel
I Don't Wanna

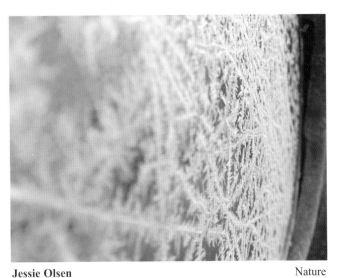

Jessie Olsen   Nature
Winter Crystals

Christopher O'Neal Collins   Portraiture
Hands Of Unity

Christopher Morgan Steward   Nature
South Haven Sunset

Aaron Shea Nicholson   Other
August

Rebecca E. Mabra   Nature
Texas Purple Cone Flower

Juliana Lucia Ivelja   People
Memory

Angie Elder   Animals/Pets
In Loving Memory Of Our Pet

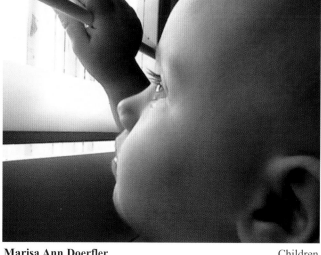

Marisa Ann Doerfler   Children
Discovering The World

J. P. Edward La Bruyere   Portraiture
La Pobre Vieja

Anthony John Marzullo   Nature
Before The Storm

Joshua Dean Hatfield   Nature
Coastal Stream

Brittlynn Rose Hoofman   Nature
In The Heavens

Tristen R. Murchie   Other
Freeway Section

Kristi Ann Knoblauch   People
Mallorie

Diane Kay Hostetler   Nature
Walkway To Paradise

Monte Goodyk   Children
Siblings In Waves

Kathi Flury   Animals/Pets
My Little Mitzi

Beth Kranick   Animals/Pets
Attitude

Austin Robert Hittel　　　　　　　　　Nature
Six In The Morning At Oxbow Bend

Jackie Autrey　　　　　　　　　Nature
Great Smoky Mountains

Dan Alan Crosley　　　　　　　　　Nature
Moss, Glenn Falls

Bernd Bartelt　　　　　　　　　Travel
The Light At Barnagat

Andy Dale　　　　　　　　　Nature
Almost Gone

Michael Hine　　　　　　　　　Nature
Man Of War—Beached

Aaron Christmas Woodard   Nature
Fly High, We Are The Sun

Megan Leigh Calcaterra   People
Take Three

Robert Steve Wright   Nature
Lily Creek Mallard

Jill Melanie Ferenc   Travel
Musee D'Orsay Clock

Ali Nicole Tradonsky   People
Forever Young

Joseph Daniel Johnson   Other
Ford Mustang GT

Raeleen Marlowe   People
I Love My Baby Dean

Kelsey Jaye Hamilton   Other
Rediscovered

Benjamin Parks Walker   Nature
Autumn Blaze

Ariana DeNevi Weckstein   People
Man On Venice Beach

Nichole E. Kytlica   Children
Innocence

Carl Enriquez   Nature
Pacific Sunset Paradise

Kristie Ann Dewell   Children
Happiness Is A Tractor Ride

Philippa Redfern   Nature
Summer Days

Susann Bergstrom   Travel
Perspective Of Love

Nicholas Floyd Robbs   Other
Country Sunset

Michael Coats   Nature
Athabasca Glacier

Kathy Lynn Dennis   Nature
Majestic

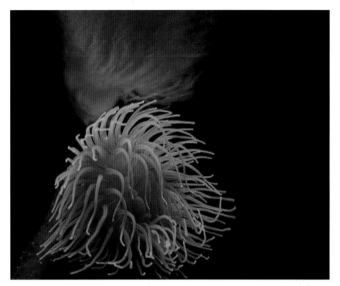

Liz M. Law Animals/Pets
Reflection

Tessa Ann Zeller Other
Faith In Yesterday

Misty Dawn Terry Nature
My Garden

Missy Kay Hansen People
Baby Blues

Holly Ann Usherwood Nature
Tranquility

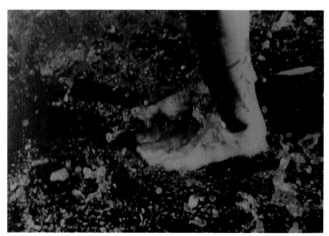

Tiffany Lazette Hertel People
Feet

Samantha Janay White   Other
Light Of Faith

Joshua J. C. Wait   Nature
Misty Harbor

Cathy Marie Fontenot   Children
Summertime Cutie

Elizabeth Anne Milton   Other
Love And Loss

Angelia M. Young   Travel
Quiescent

Shintaro Nambu   Animals/Pets
The Sweetest Squirrel

Brittney Hoppa Animals/Pets
Ms. Coco

Caitlin Patricia Grieve Other
Desolation

Stefanie A. Joseph People
Transcendence

Jaclyn Beth Donges Nature
Serenity

Robert Klaus Sall Nature
Hidden Treasures

John W. Brown People
Untitled

Jessica Renee Bloomer   Other
Retired Worker

Amanda Elsie Shellnut   People
Mommy's Big Day

Melissa Ann Gianfalla   Other
Reflections Of Naturel Beauty

Elizabeth Blanche Ito   People
The Perfect Hunter, Can't Ask For Another!

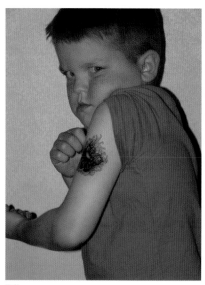

Barbara L. Riley   Children
Trouble With A Capital "T"

Charlesty Misty Burchfield   Children
Short Walks In The Park

Brandon Maurice Tyler   Nature
A Son's Farewell

Sharon Wells   Children
Mini Me!

Benjamin Eric Bellavance   Nature
Sky From Davis Mountain

Zanetta A. Barnes   Nature
Endless Quest For Tranquility

Marci Lynne Morris   Travel
Nighttime Reflections

Allen Farnham   Nature
Sunset Star

Trevor John Milevskiy   Nature
Wet Snow

Alison H. Lamm   Nature
Through The Trees

Martha M. Stout   Nature
Bee And Butterfly

Donna Gail Hearndon   Nature
Autumn In The Smoky Mountains

Alex Dappen   Action
Whistler Whip

Jarrod A. Sams   Nature
Autumn Torches

Bonnie Lu Seymour   People
T. J.

Alison Hyatt   Nature
Fields Of Gold

Christina Schoch   Other
Descent

Brittany Sabrina Parker   Animals/Pets
Humming In Mexico

Mary Elizabeth Brunst   Animals/Pets
Uninhibited Play

David Avery Leiserson   People
Across The Bay

Jennifer Susan Burdick   Children
Emma Love

Daniel Ruvalcaba   Children
You Came From Where?

Andrew Louis Stacy   Nature
Fall Branch Falls

Kyle Troy Stewart   Travel
Stonehenge Sunset

Geoffrey D. Brown   People
A Night With Aui

Robert Dale Gladden   Nature
Golden Gate Bridge

Lisa Rayel Fields　　　　　　　　　Nature
Dahliance

Terri Lynn Shepke　　　　　　　　Animals/Pets
Teddy Lynn Shepke

Cherie Mortensen　　　　　　　　Nature
Capitol Reflection

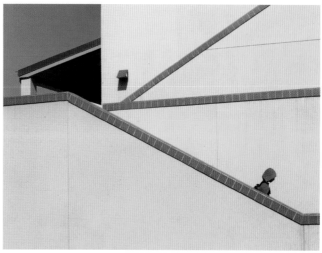

Guillermo Enrique Amador　　　　　Children
Hope

Dean Andrew Van Zyl　　　　　　Nature
Lily In Afternoon Light

Jessica Alice Watson　　　　　　　Travel
Contemplation

Steven Raper   Children
Lane, Our Miracle

Michelle Helen Brockman   Nature
Through Folded Leaves

Bobby D. Criswell   Nature
New Beginning

Tina Beckman   Travel
The Big Blue Escape

Vickie L. McClure   Nature
Reflections

Pam K. Kazamer image:

Pam K. Kazamer   Children
My First Dance

Carlon Porche Mangrum   Sports
Barefooting The Locks In Talisheek, Louisiana

James Edward Tompkins   Nature
Limitless Grace

Kehley R. Shank   Action
P. B. A. Fire

Joseph C. Donilon   People
Man's Best Friend

Subhankar Sarkar   Sports
The Trainee And The Trainer

Nadezda Pavlovna Schellhorn   People
Alisa

Michael Newman   Animals/Pets
Banjo

Tom Pangborn   Nature
The Maine Cabin Guardian

Suzanne Gail Crane   Nature
High Water

Jordon Adidas Mach   Other
Sound Check

Natasha Melissa Mathias   Nature
Mating Eagles

Jerry L. Gadd   Nature
Paired For Life

Cindy Lynn Caulfield Travel
The Essence Of Ireland

Sarah Plummer Nature
Red Flower In Spokane

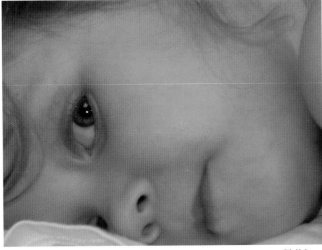

Melissa Green Children
A Moment In Time

Brandy Sue Ackerson Children
Perseverance

Amanda Kate Dillard Other
Holding On For Life

Joan Baker Nature
Florida Sunset

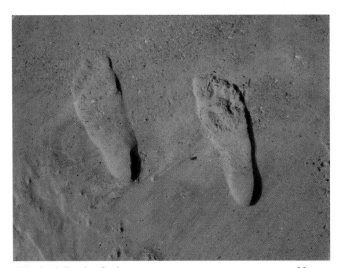

Elizabeth Benita Smit   Nature
Footprints In The Sand

Jason Edward Horace Wade   Action
Sky High

Melinda Karen Marshall   Nature
Clouds: God's Artwork

Lynsey Olson   Nature
Blue Ridge Parkway Sunrise

Michael David Kenny   Nature
Amidst Mountain And Sky

Tracy Pecor   Animals/Pets
Callie

Rich Reese Nature
Morning Dew

Heather S. Ramler Nature
Costa Rican Shore

Tamara Krueger Children
Girls Rule

Carlos Ezekiel Ze-Dukes People
Zebraknight Zebra—Cup Of Music

Tessa Kathleen Owen Portraiture
Morning Ride

Emily Ann Isakson Action
Free Falling

James Alan Guth   Nature
Nature's Fall Magic

Brian James Milliken   Nature
Summer On The Saco River

Rikki Erin Levine   People
Out Of The Box

Rachel Ze Thompson   Animals/Pets
Never Smile At A Crocodile

Catherine M. Haskett   Animals/Pets
Bear Raspberry

Samantha Holly Miller   Nature
Alaska

Michael Bryan Metcalf   Travel
St. Isaac's Sunrise

Heather A. Busing   Portraiture
Beautiful Girl

Nancy Emery Young   Portraiture
Lost In Song

Eric Anderson   Animals/Pets
Ohio Bird

Stephanie Alexandra Lucente   People
Mother And Child

Anne Marie Shifley   Animals/Pets
Untitled

Grant E. Fairbrun   Nature
Serenity

Kyle Patrick Tyson   Nature
Winter Wonderland

Karl E. Van Leishout   Nature
A Bee's Dream

Colleen Joyce Villeneuve   Children
My Boys

Catalina Piedrahita   Other
Paint And Skin

Megan Bodart   Animals/Pets
Fighting Grizzly Bears

Sydney K. Helland Nature
Tingling

Charlotte N. Pringle Nature
Sunset With A Bird

Joseph Hart Haberl Nature
Night Destroys The Day

Kristine Lynn Buchholtz Nature
Autumn In Christchurch

Thomas Ward Other
Splash

Ana Christina Oliveira Nature
Sea Painting

Shelley Ann Hunlin Nature
A Ray Of Sunshine

Andy M. Hanson People
Walking In Mexico

Heidi Nicole Veldhuizen Portraiture
Romanticized Serenity

Dawn Maier Nature
Carolina Garden

Rachel Marie Hill Other
Cadence

Emma Marshane Taylor Children
Emma Sleeping

Summer Mae Underwood Nature
Cunningham Falls

Keith Andrew Trepanier Travel
Turning Point

Mandy Elissa Ruble Nature
Up In The Sky

Jacquelyn R. Piper Children
Lucy's Wait

Angel Leah Jones Animals/Pets
Kentucky Fields

Hope Ogunbamiyo Children
Peek-A-Boo

Varun Poddar　　　　　　　　　　Animals/Pets
Bird Watching

Kyle M. Robillard　　　　　　　　Action
Skate—New York City

Kasi G. Rink　　　　　　　　　　Nature
Sunset

Erin Shapiro　　　　　　　　　　Other
In The Dark

Karim Pierre Gharios　　　　　　Travel
Dubai

Whitney Leigh Mayer　　　　　　Other
Night Lights

Jaci Elizabeth Hammill People
Water Fights

Kate Luvera Nature
Fighting Off The Weeds

Jessi Lyn Teaff People
Perspective

Kendra May Davis Nature
Trees

Jody Lynn Jobson Nature
Night Lily

Matthew Allen Werther Nature
Sunset Beach

Megan Emily Mihalich Travel
Paris Aglow

Diane Marie Knepp Animals/Pets
Australian Sea Lions At Play

Tammy Elizabeth Beckman Nature
Landscape Of Rosehill Cemetery

Jeannie M. Benson Animals/Pets
Max

Samuel Wren Bendall People
Inspiration

Maggie Mae Wallace Nature
Big Meadows

Benthe Ljostad Rolfsen　　　　　　　Animals/Pets
Here I Come

Richard Paul Posluszny　　　　　　　Other
Eyes To New York City

Jackie Ferko　　　　　　　Animals/Pets
Wet Nose

Michael Paul Clawson　　　　　　　Children
Come On, Just One Kiss

Daniel Michael McNeil　　　　　　　Animals/Pets
Just Another Day

Jennifer L. Bermudez　　　　　　　Other
In The Night

Maria Stergiou   People
Your Call Is Being Diverted

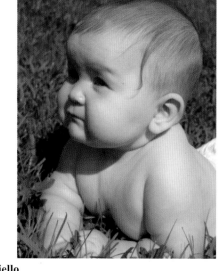

Leslie Aiello   People
Thoughts

Laura Kay Stunkel   Portraiture
Empty Jack

Kim Malone   Nature
What A View

Brittany Lyn Mario   Nature
Summer Love

Brenton John Mallen   Nature
For You

Kristen Leigh Kreefer   Children
Rotten!

Megan Elizabeth Pollard   Nature
Beauty In Construction

Sarah Nicole Pope   Nature
Fish Creek

Francie Whitlow   Nature
Spillway

Sonja Michele Edwards   Children
Emma And Her Big Sis, Kylee

Tong Nguyen   Animals/Pets
Spider

Farida N. Basha
On Our Way To Algiers

Nature

Camille Joy Penner
Petal

Nature

Joel Eli Johnston
Two Free Boys

Children

Leigh-Ann Chase Hoets
Beauty In The Bush

Nature

Tina Louise Corby
Smithy

People

Michael Li
Happiness

People

Tina Picard Travel
Sunset Over Water

Mark Alan Benner Nature
Moonlight Eagle

Sherri Higginbotham Nature
Iris In My Eye

Amy Marie Chapman Children
Ana Banana

Lewis Tieman Jr. Nature
A Pink Seagull

Molly Joy Cunningham Children
Flower Child

Angela G. DeLeal   Other
Grandpa's Birdhouse

Giovanni Fontana   Children
Dreaming

Judith Penny   Nature
Morning Stream

Deanna Lynn Ward   Nature
Perfect Beauty

Desiree Star Johnson-Garrard   Animals/Pets
The Bear

Bree Celeste Christiansen   Nature
Sunset At Thunder Lake

Joanne Beverly Collard   Nature
Summer Lilies

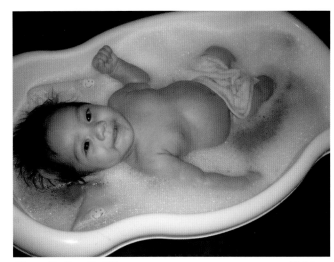

Chantelle Rae Padilla   Children
Tiny Bubble

Kirsty Vandenburg   Travel
Less Is More

Eugene Riggs   Other
Morning

Kathleen M. Jones   Travel
The Way Home

Jenna M. Coon   Other
All Washed Up

Krystal Dawn Gray   Portraiture
Graduation

Marjorie Schultze   Nature
Stepping Stone

Jo Grossman   Other
Pathway

Jason Rydquist   People
Sunflower Dream

Russell Ellise Robinson   Children
Eating Out

Luisa Cruz   People
Man Alone

Vanessa Lara Hernandez   Children
Noah

Janice Marie Nelson   Nature
Sensual Sunrise

Grant Lamont   Nature
Just Hanging Around

John Kossitch   Nature
Baby Birds

Sherry Jo Stevens   Animals/Pets
Sitting Pretty

Andrew Leroy Simmering   Nature
Monumental

Michael Robert Bull　　　　　　　Nature
Summer Sunrise

Gina K. Arzaga　　　　　　　Travel
Train

Ryleigh Paige McKlemurry　　　　　　　Children
Mini Me

Gayle M. Nagle　　　　　　　Children
I Pledge Allegiance

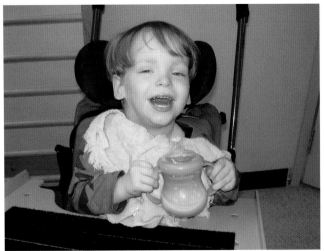

Kim Carole Drozdyk　　　　　　　Children
No Limits For C. P. Children

Challaine Morgan Emerson　　　　　　　Travel
Mexican Beauty

Krystal Marie Henderson   Nature
Solitude

Rebekka Lea White   Children
Unforgettable Moments

Tanya Tungilik   Nature
Tarraq

Monalisa Salib   Nature
Beyond The Doors

Leslie Lynn Sultemeier   Travel
The Ice Climber

Elaine Beaudoin   Nature
Crowsnest Mountain Through The Clouds

Erin Elizabeth Cox   Nature
Winter Solitude

Gloria Jean Furgason   Nature
Bug Checking Out The World

Douglas Johnson   Children
Child's Play

Linda Rose Chilcott   Nature
Lake

Tyson Ray Bradley   People
J. D. And Me

Herman Ordonez   Travel
Untitled

Karolyn W. Stuver Travel
Greek Work Boat

Jessica L. Gerrish Other
Halcyon

Shanna Lynn Claborn Other
Goo Tube

Maria Victoria Koon Children
Baby Connor Showing New Teeth

Robert P. Johnston People
Wrestling In The Snow

Silvina Salazar Animals/Pets
Just Turn Around

Aaron Schwartz　　　　　　　　　　　Nature
Above The Clouds

Lina Campos Shellhorn　　　　　　　Nature
Black Mountains, Arizona

Maryana Beletskaya　　　　　　　　　Travel
Ferrara

Andrea Palacios　　　　　　　　　　　Nature
Caldera

Simon C. Ross　　　　　　　　　　　Travel
Tram Gate

Ashley Ann Anderson　　　　　　　　Other
The Road To New Orleans

Melinda Sue Ybarra Animals/Pets
Baby Goat

Erin Leigh Duff People
Calming Daisies

Mandi G. Lauser Nature
Hot Spring Winter

Dana Marie Rakoci Nature
Fall In The Smoky Mountains

Jim W. Lindsay Travel
Purple Majesty

Jonathan Jason Kabas Portraiture
Midway Series

Randall Kohl Bowden   Nature
Leave Your Mark

M-J S. Sapinsky   Animals/Pets
Kermode Bear

Louis William Kunstek   Animals/Pets
Hawk—Silent Predator

Alyssa McMahon   Nature
Morning Beaches In British Columbia

Kelly James Tarala   Children
Peek-A-Boo

Christopher Jackson   Nature
Rock And Mountain Scene

Melonie Anne Calam   Animals/Pets
Feral Kittens—Willow, Fairy, And Grub

Robin Carol Ruby   Action
Boy Running On Beach

Sarah Christine Huff   Animals/Pets
Lizard Shadow

Saskia Quinn Jacobson   Travel
Bridges In Amsterdam

Whitney Jean Bergum   Nature
Finding Faith

Rebecca Lynn Harper   Animals/Pets
Fall Furry

Tara Louise Eldred   Other
Mother Mary

Jeannette Maryanne Baxter   Nature
Island Paradise

Michaela J. Wiens   Nature
Kalamalka

Joshua B. Garner   Nature
Sunset Over Indigo Marina

Brian Mathew Blostica   Nature
Drive To The Old Barn

Karen Fletcher   Nature
Orange Sunset

Karen Lynn Bunda   Nature
Eagle Cloud

Sandy Nanod Long   Nature
Loreneo

Jason Vladinir Halliburton   Other
Sweet, Sexy Serenity

Lisa-May Crowther   Animals/Pets
High-Speed Crossing

David Alfio Nicotra   Nature
Blue Beauty

Lilit Petrosyan   Children
Baby Santa

Aaron James Atkinson   Other
City Bridge

Jenn Pedro   Nature
Sunshine Ocean

Paul Sheffrin   Nature
Lonely Reed

Wendy Gudmundson   Nature
Vision From Above

David Layne Ward   Nature
Untitled

Helen Peng   Other
I Give You My Heart

Sandy Allyne Wells　　　　Nature
Sunset At The Ranch

Hilda Bernadine Tennisco　　　　Children
Precious Emma

Dulcey H. Fuqua　　　　Other
Inspired

Benjamin D. Banker　　　　People
What's Next?

Daniel E. Newton　　　　Portraiture
First Tattoo

Mary Ann Waite　　　　Nature
Timeless Beauty

Ken J. Clark   Nature
Nature At Its Best

Marcia K. Foreman   Other
Side By Side

Ken Smith   Humor
Who's The Boss?

Lisa Beth Arion   Animals/Pets
Innocent Till Proven Guilty

Ramiz Pasic   Travel
Streets Of Oaxaca, Mexico

Amy M. Cox   Children
Innocence

Kayleigh Victoria Pool　　　　　　　　　　Animals/Pets
Best Friends

Marilyn Ann Dowling　　　　　　　　　　Nature
Serenity

Cassaundra E. Chiu　　　　　　　　　　Other
Reaching For The Top

Teresa Ann Daniels　　　　　　　　　　Nature
God's In The Details

Debora Lynn Kummer　　　　　　　　　　Nature
Lake Louise

James Michael Demboski　　　　　　　　　　Nature
Winter Solace

Rebecca Anne Burton Other
A Lifestyle Forgotten

Cherry Nicole Mathis People
Mama's Little Blossom

Nick Crneckiy Nature
Nature's Many Paths

Blake Andrew Nellis Travel
St. Paul's Eye

Phil Weinisch Nature
The Hand Of Mother Nature

Emma Louise Holt Other
Night Skies

Maribeth Zuesi-Kreu   Nature
Gorilla—Pittsburgh Zoo

Sandra Peszek   Children
Matthew Melts Your Heart

Andrew Ka Ho Cheng   Travel
Stanley

Wendy Jo Ellis   Children
Christmas Magic

Carly Anna Andrahovitch   Nature
Climb Up The Tree

Gary W. Wilkie   Nature
Autumn Basket

Tarah Annlouise Sackett   Children
Playtime In The Winter

Paul Terence Green   People
Chobe Twilight

Sandy Dee Fullen   Nature
Total Bliss

Kenneth Lee LaFrance   Travel
Space Needle In Seattle, Washington

Paul Daniel Creurer   Nature
Muppet On A Stick

Cheryl Walker   Nature
Pink Light

72

Karen Ann Arender   Children
So Happy

Trish Newman   Travel
The Mystical Machu Picchu, Peru

Troy Alan Hattermann   Travel
Ponte Vecchio

Linda Toborowsky   Animals/Pets
William

Eduardo Veguilla   Animals/Pets
Yawn!

Sandra Lee Welch   Travel
San Francisco's High Steel

Michele Hagedus Children
Stevie

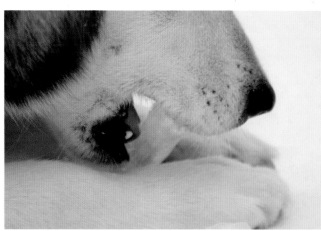

Jennifer McNaughton Animals/Pets
Auroro's Icicle

Jenny Ellen Von Flatern Travel
The Grand Canyon

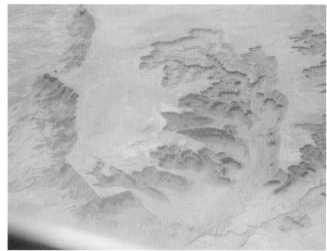

Michelle E. Kirkland Travel
Utah Canyons From The Sky

Michael Cloutier Nature
Bridge To Serenity

Julie Beasley Tyler Children
Star Gazer

Tanya Weber   Children
Content

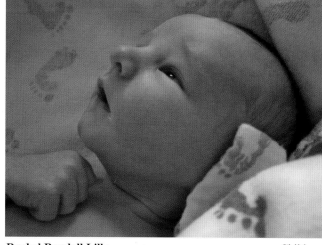

Rachel Randall Lilly   Children
My Sweet Angel

Louise Kathleen Mabon   Children
Playing In Sunshine

Greg Pascut   Animals/Pets
Peace In A Wasteland

James J. Bos   Nature
Michigan Winter Sun

Crystal L. Snelbaker   Children
Lila Plays Peek-A-Boo

Terry Charles Studd Children
Alberta's Favorite Pastime

Evangeline Gaudiosa Anacleto Animals/Pets
Sharing

Joshua Mark Lutz Nature
America's Front Yard

Jenna M. Kendrick Children
A Child's Autumn

Patrick James Bone Travel
Beautiful Lake

Peter Joseph Biancani Nature
Autumn Spirit

Amanda Katherine Gruenloh   Other
The Little Moments

Cherita Ann Adams   Children
Jolie And Dallen

Deana Skidmore   Nature
Journeys

Carrie Ann Coursolle   Children
Cast A Shadow Over Me

Shaun Perry Grein   Sports
Middle Of Training

David W. Falconieri   People
Last Farewell

Leah Jade Emmerson People
Maybe

Stefano Buliani Animals/Pets
There's A Snake Lurking In The Grass

Stephanie Lydie Jones Children
Watching The Birds

Thomas R. Catron Action
Patrolling The Streets Of Iraq

Patrick Palmer Other
La Porte

Nicole Marie O'Neill People
Praise Me

Madeleine Christine Bilodeau　　　　　　Nature
Fantastic Dawn

Max L. Owen　　　　　　Animals/Pets
My Pool

Joe Dimattia　　　　　　People
Elegant Mischief

Noella Bujold　　　　　　Nature
Live Oaks

Maxim Denis Siebert　　　　　　Nature
A Lovely Sunset

Carla LeAnn Spradling　　　　　　Nature
Fall's Bright Bloom

April G. I. M. Young   Nature
A Timeless Moment

Shelby Payton Medin   Other
Musicality

Madeleine Rose Beaton   Nature
Waking Life

Lauren Leona Schmenk   Nature
Soft Landing

Melissa Mae Gardiner   Animals/Pets
Backyard Visitor

Jamie Lee Graham   Children
Wrangler Butts!

Alison H. Hunt   Portraiture
Ella

Jesse James Connolly   Nature
Wisps

Ben Adams   Other
All In A Day's Work

Linda Jean Hemsworth   Travel
Lake McKenzie, Fraser Island, Queensland

Michael-Francis Kelly   Nature
Sydney Sunrise

Michelle Ann Henderson   Animals/Pets
Sunset's Echo

Dave M. Yocke   Nature
Murmuring Brook

Nicholas Alonzo Hersey   Nature
Our Love Is A Waterfall

Scott T. E. Cooper   Nature
Tranquility

Tosha Ann Kidd   Travel
Reflection

Greg A. Chaney   Action
Qualifying Runs

Myrtle Jean Palmer   Travel
High Flight

Lauren K. Studley   People
Mike At Atsuta Jingu Shrine

Morris Cunningham   Nature
Road Block

Cory Jade Nemeth   Other
Shaded City

Nicole M. Lemke   Nature
Finding Africa In Vancouver

Dina Ann Chirico   Travel
Passage

Jay Patrick Mohan   Animals/Pets
Duck Hunt

Mikael Matias Takamaa   Nature
The End Of A Perfect Day!

Jonathan Ashley Atamaniuk   Other
Night Park

Anya Alyssa Ciesienski   Other
Drip

Patrick George Rocheleau   Other
Imprisoned

Diana L. Whiteley   Travel
Simon Says, "Assisi"

Duncan Allen Patton   Nature
Vanishing Footprints

Vivian Leigh Gilmore   People
Amber

Julie A. Demas   People
1, 2, 3, Smile!

Jane Laura Bennett   Other
Melbourne From The Spirit Of Taz

Rebecca Whorton   Children
Tyler

Donna Foster Myer   Nature
Miss Lily—Heading Home

Corey D. Johnson   People
Corey Johnson

Donald John Begg   Animals/Pets
Snow Geese

Ann Marie Burt   Nature
Tree Frog

Barbara B. Hajek   Other
On The Farm

Joy Kingsbury   Portraiture
Thoughtful Gaze

Harry M. Platcow   Travel
Vegas Venetian

Vicky I. Long   Nature
Birds Of Paradise

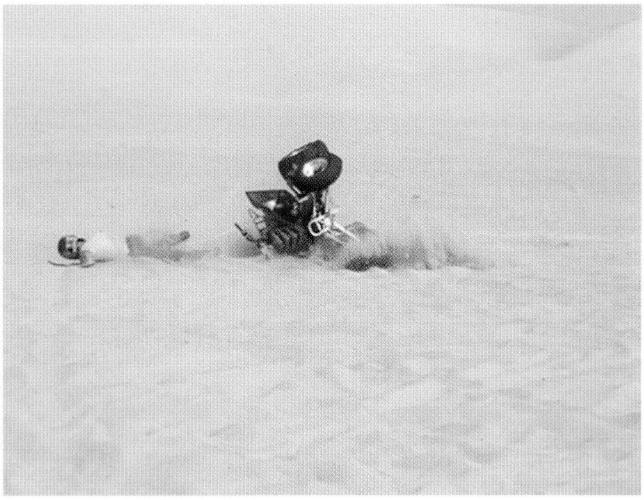

Seileen P. Wood Sports
Karma At Its Best

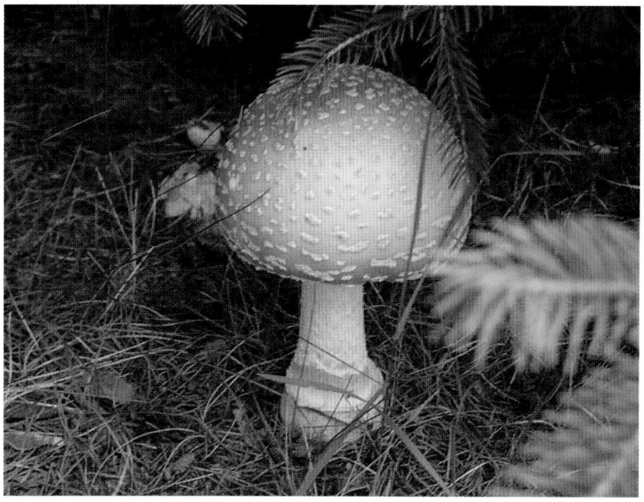

Holly Ruth Siczkar Nature
Mom's Mushroom

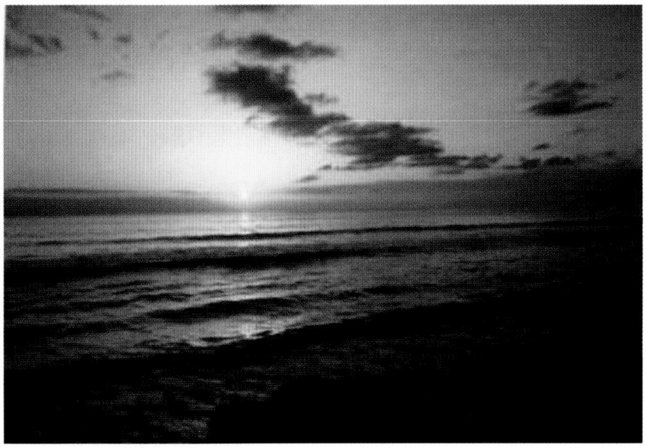

Vivian Belinda Mirabal Other
Serenity

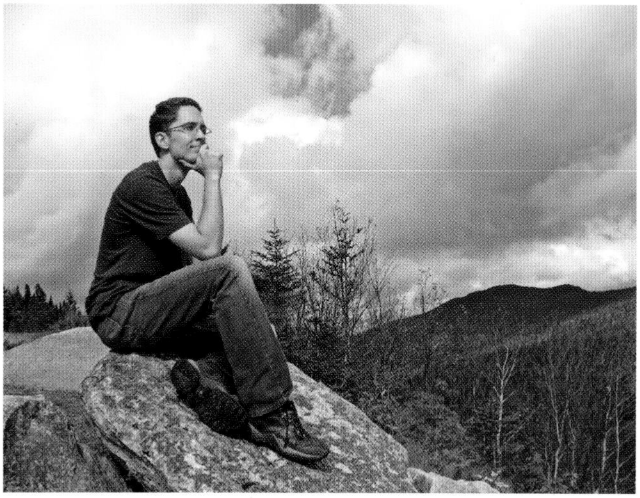

Rachelle Gauthier Nature
Contemplation

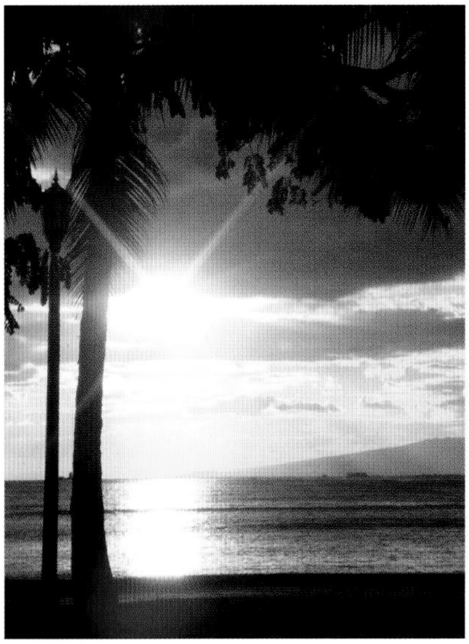

Andrea Lynn Visocsky Nature
Romantic Hawaiian Sunset

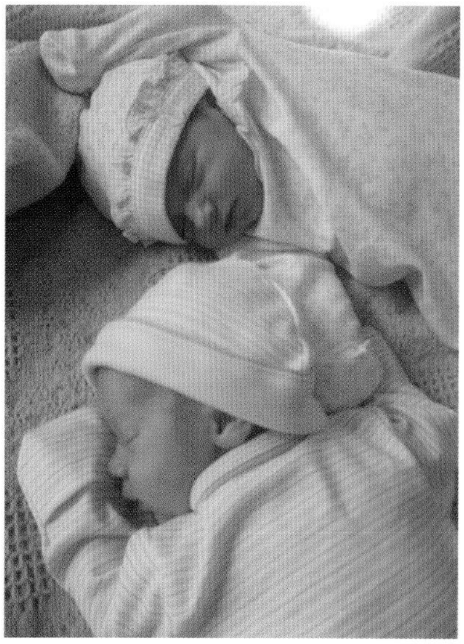

Tara Beth Lucosky Children
Sleeping Angels

Tara Diane O'Roark Nature
Dock Of The Bay

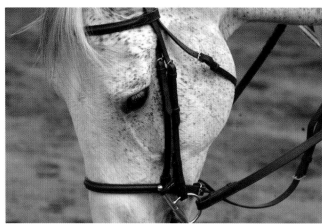

Ashley Payge Devine Animals/Pets
Del-Mar

Imeleta Tatiana Chancheck Children
Lucky, I Love Hawaii

Laurie Cudahy Nature
Running With The Wind

Tim David Newberry Animals/Pets
Untitled

Boki Jerinic Other
Pinery Park

Ken V. Plumbly   Other
Fogoten And Alone

Brenda Nelson   Children
My Little Cowgirl

Jessica Poulos   Other
The Paper Crane

Deletha Sowells   Children
A Day In The Cotton Patch

Jason Ronald Romero   Animals/Pets
Handsomely Happy

Darcy Kennedy   Children
In Deep Thought

Cheryl Lutman   Children
Knee Deep In Smiles

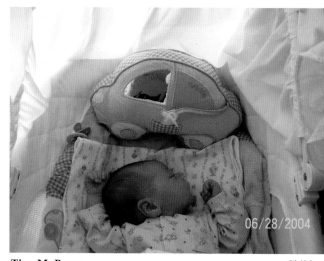

Tina M. Perez   Children
Sweet Little Boy

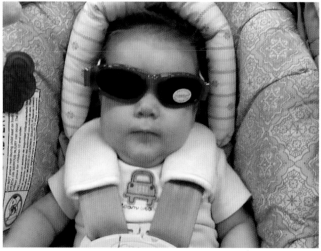

Kerry Hoisington   Children
Grandson

Michael Todd Shull   Children
A Day At The Park

Alina Kandinova   Other
Keepsakes

Ronald J. Hatton   Nature
Lake Francis

Emily Wasiuk   Animals/Pets
Happy Valentine's Day

Tammy Denise Emon   Nature
Asiatic Lily Cordelia

Jodi Marie Brunner   Portraiture
Saw

Sky Alice Loth   Other
Pathways

Joshua Freedman   Other
Golden Sunrise

Colin K. Prasad   Travel
The Breath Of The South Pacific

Haider Quazi Wasim   Nature
Never-Ending Beauties

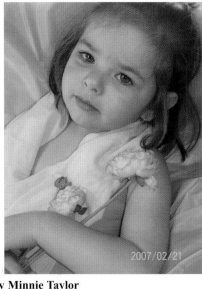

Sarah Dolly Minnie Taylor   Children
Precious Memories

Jeffrey John Shea   Animals/Pets
Badger

Rekha Joshi   Children
Mischieviously Thoughtful

Nikki Lynn Walker   People
Nikki Lynn Walker

Jennie Theresa Straughan   Nature
Serenity

Lisa-Marie Proteau   Other
Dying To Go Left

Jaymie Silken Karn   Nature
Look On The Bright Side

Alex Orlove Dilley   Nature
Valley Forge Sunset

Peter J. Eyrich   Other
Reflections

Mark Joseph Lane   People
Alicia

Erik Anders Michael Haake   Portraiture
Down

Keith W. Forrest   People
My Little Dutchy

Darlene Ann Demars   Nature
Autumn Serenity

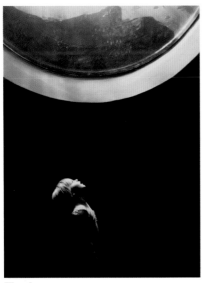

Seth James Floyd   Children
Wondermant At Aquarium

Christina Jane Sawisky   Nature
Still Stance

Cheryl D. Fisher   Nature
Red Beauty

Kim C. Cordeiro   Humor
Which Way To Go?

Karolina Katarzyna Turek People
Sunset Jane

Tommy Burton Walsh Animals/Pets
Magnificent Habitat

Daniel Tardif Travel
A Poet's Journey

Cindy Lynn Veroline Nature
Smile, God Loves You

Lourdes Garibay Children
Walking At The Beach

Tara Jenkins Nature
Foggy Sunrise

Kaye Alison Clarke   Nature
Sunrise

Blandye J. Crawford   Children
Summer Fun

Chantal Mary Davis   Animals/Pets
Hideaway

Katie McInroy   Travel
An Italian Afternoon

Sarah Nicole Martin   Other
Stairway To Heaven

Brian S. Frank   Nature
Take Me To Your Leader

Jordan Parker   Nature
Milford Sound

Mark Robert Scione Jr.   Nature
Dusk

Jenn K. Trueman   Nature
Summer Nights

Jo Ann Collins   Children
Blue Maggie

Francisco Soucy   Travel
Coucher De Lune A Biarritz

John K. Sampson   Nature
What's Next?

Patricia Gillingham Britton　　　　　Nature
Spring Fawn

Trina Rose Marie Borgerding　　　　　Portraiture
Mitchell Posing

Cathy L. Randazzo　　　　　Nature
Morning Dew Web

Sandra Lee Sommerfield　　　　　People
Oh, Boy, I'm With My Daddy

Jessica Marie Johnston　　　　　Travel
Aloha States

Carrie J. Gati　　　　　Children
The Pumpkin Patch Boys

Norm Dunn Nature
Path Through Nature

Ashlee Amanda Kivell People
Trapped In Shadows

Charlotte Afonsa Rattray Children
Charlotte Afonso Rattray—Boo-Boo Bear

Carol Grenier Nature
One So Different, But Beautiful

Linda Ellenberger Travel
Sunrise In Alaska

Arthur H. Krueger Action
Flight

Brittany M. Parrish Animals/Pets
Playful Pup

Penny Anne O'Donnell People
Best Friends

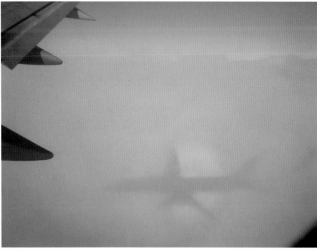

Kathy A. Carr Travel
Up In The Clouds

Charles Michael Hughes Nature
Moon Set

Jaime E. Guzman Animals/Pets
Nap Dog

Kaye Elizabeth Frost-Smith Sports
Fisherman's Transport

Amy Lauren Lohman   Nature
Up In The Clouds

Jennifer Stewart   Animals/Pets
A'Isha And Her Dog

Whitney Nicole Harper   Children
Hand In Hand

Terry Yopp   Children
Mmm-Mmm Good

Erik Bentley Roomet   Nature
Untitled

Sarah Ann Siedsma   Nature
Peace Among Nature

Tania L. Sederlan   Nature
Memory

Mary Doris MacDougall   Nature
Sunset In Cape Breton

Jamie Estelle Moore   Nature
Rotten Fruit

Linda Charlene Crouch   Travel
Pei

Caleb J. Shortt   Sports
Old School

Debbie Alice Teufel   Animals/Pets
King Of My Jungle

Ronette B. Thompson　　　　People
Double The Beauty

Stephanie Rita-Anne Markel　　　　Travel
Chicago Parking

Brian Kent Page　　　　Animals/Pets
Brothers

Pelin Gul　　　　Nature
My Little Hole Of Peace

Lori S. Rains　　　　Travel
Silent Fall

Carrie Ann Scott　　　　People
Shootin' The Breeze

Cynthia McCloskey People
Wink

Sara Faye Hall Children
Apple Of My Eye

Shelly May Bell Other
Canada Day

Gayle Van Nort Animals/Pets
Are We There Yet?

Alexander Daniel Sanderson Nature
Sunset Reflection

Tracey J. Hardesty Nature
Butterfly

Candy Sue Ferguson   Children
It's My Party And I'll Eat All The Cake I Want

Jarrad Duggan   Travel
Santa Monica

Cassandra Leigh Frankham   Nature
Nighttime Skies

Angie Marie Shults   Animals/Pets
After A Long Hard Day

Nicole Lee Drew   Nature
Fresh Cut

Gregory Allen King   Animals/Pets
Rascal

Augustina Finch   Other
Dove In The Sky

Cynthia Marie Herndon   Animals/Pets
Christmas Pups

Clayton L. Parker   Action
Sea World

Kevin S. Patterson   Animals/Pets
Freedom Icon

Diane Lynn Richie   Children
High Five

Brad James Clay   Nature
Just Another Day

Lindsey Kristine Johnson　　　　　　　　Portraiture
Glasses

Clayton Haner　　　　　　　　Other
Night On The Street

Randi Amber Anthony　　　　　　　　Nature
Catching Some Rays

Kolya Nicolay Hicker　　　　　　　　Animals/Pets
My Dog, Sammy, And I

Andre Jones　　　　　　　　Nature
Beautiful

Matthew Brian Crooks　　　　　　　　Nature
Summer Bloom

Svetlana G. Orekhova-Tibbits   People
Boy's Mama Is In Iraq

Traci Kaye Mongan   Portraiture
Motherly Love

Hanieh Okhovat   Other
Funeral

Vince Golea   People
Look Into My Eye

Colleen Margaret Curran   Nature
Mexico Beauty

Kaili Metsala   Animals/Pets
The Blossom Of Friendship

Danny Sipiora Animals/Pets
Eddie

Pam Nicole Nicholson Nature
Calm Water

Adam N. Howard Travel
Eiffel Flower

Jeffrey Alan Mellgren Nature
Sunset On Lake Waconia

Simon James Layng Other
Foggy Morning In Nunavut

Stacey Breanne Collison Nature
Crazy Busy Nature

Katie Elizabeth Stewart   Other
To Pass The Time

Ashley Catherine Vondervoort   Animals/Pets
Creatures Of The Wild

Urszula Barbara Stratton   Animals/Pets
Day At The Zoo

James Richard Neale   Action
London Bus

Chelsea Brienna Herbert   Nature
Over The Edge

Hollie Dawn Marks   Nature
Serenity

Rose Faro   Nature
Big Red Oak

Brigit Wood   Nature
Day Is Done

Carolyne Margaret Woodley-Cardy   Nature
Buy This House

Ben George Clifford   Children
Soggy Cereal

Ingrid Avendano-Quinones   Children
Candy, What Candy?

Dale Arnold   People
Untitled

Aaron Micheal Weleschuk Nature
Butterfly

Donald Baldwin Travel
Lighthouse

Sherri A. Richardson Portraiture
Teen And Her Dog

Lora H. Kane Animals/Pets
Cat

Julia Russell Travel
Sunset Over Scicli

Courtney Marie Coffin People
Bittersweet

Twylia J. Sekavec   Children
My First Rifle

Kajoli Khanna   People
Shadows

Maritza Barbara Martinez   Nature
Atardecer En Sur De Tenerife

Terri W. Eash   Children
Can You Say No To This Face?

Haewon Cho   Nature
Twilight Of The Gods

Cindy Lea Schubert   Animals/Pets
Cheap Acting Lessons

Miles Coleman Rouse   Sports
Night-Flow

Jessica Marie Pranskevich   Nature
Heaven

Marjorie Ann Nejman   Travel
Give Me A Reason To Stay

Ji-yun Yuna Yoon   Other
Art Shop In Downtown

Matt Sayles   Nature
Nature's Surreality

Julie Marie Arturo   Nature
Natural-Born Model

Jake Wolseley Latham   Other
Robert's Quest

Rachel Ann Peterson   Children
Generation Gap

Zach Elliott Wengrovius   Nature
Above The Fog

Maciej Swieboda   People
True Love

Alan J. Haley   Children
Sisters At Sunset

Carissa Zavada   Nature
Symbiotic Perspective

Neil Clive Chislett   Travel
Amsterdam In Motion

Bryce Richardson Adams   Travel
Driven For Survival

Brooke Ann Bouchillon   Sports
Comin' At Ya

Rob Reading   Nature
Light Interrupted

Breanne Lee Ilchyna   Nature
In A Winter Dream

Jason Pierre   People
Daydream

Kelsey A. Wagner   Other
Brighten

Joan Fiander   Animals/Pets
Eagle And Otters

Hannah Jarvis   Other
Splash Of Silver

Emily Depasse   Travel
Sunset Grille

Jordy Raye Steciuk   People
Beside Her

Laurie Gayle Self   Animals/Pets
Home Improvement

Cadell L. Alexander Animals/Pets
Green Jay

Chadd Allan Murphy Animals/Pets
Shape Shifter

Crystal Lynn Nieman Children
Endless Amazement

Kimberly Ann Tate Children
Cheese!

Amber Lee Konikow Nature
A Moment In Jasper

Whitney Hughes Nature
Sky Larch

Morgana Maxine Stafford　　　　　Animals/Pets
English Robin

Arturo R. Fernandez　　　　　Travel
Inevitable Storm

Andrew Aaron Hunt　　　　　Other
Road Block

Wendy M. McRoberts　　　　　People
Bliss

Ashley Jane McKee　　　　　Animals/Pets
Snow Dog

Bryan Michael Considder　　　　　Other
World Left Behind

Brandi Lynn   Nature
Upside Down

Blair Tyler Johnston   Animals/Pets
Can I Have It?

Stefani L. Meriwether   People
A Quiet Moment In The Midst Of Summer Fun

Mike David Hoskins   Nature
A Blurred Moment In Time

Angie V. Hendrix   Nature
Another Member Of God's Air Force

Debbie Piantadosi   People
Blue On Blue—Joy

Denise Ann Stewart   Nature
Midnight Sun

Marie Geritz   Nature
Busy Bee

Victoria J. Sheldon   Nature
Night Visitor

Gaynor Jones   Animals/Pets
Listening

Melissa Rodriguez   People
Road Rage

Beth R. Jeffries   Nature
Both Sides Of Light

Kimberly Pusic   Animals/Pets
Tigger

Becky Toccoa King   Children
My Two Little Girls

Pearce David Darnell   Portraiture
Given From Above

Betsy Knapp Deis   Nature
August Storm

Gloria Jean Waite   Animals/Pets
Owl

Mischa D. Leon   Nature
Garden Delight

Sara Elizabeth Whorton   Children
Play Date

Rachel Elizabeth Sanguinito   Other
New Life

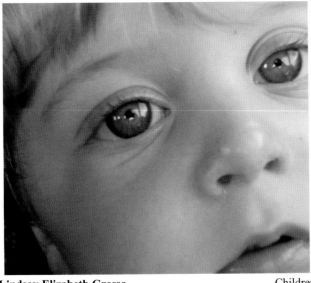

Lindsay Elizabeth Grosso   Children
Baby Blue Eyes

Christopher Phelan   Nature
Hawaii Flower

Debra Williams   Animals/Pets
Ahh, Life Is Good

Alexis A. Houser   Children
Upside-Down Summer Fun

Salena M. Catron　　　　　　Children
Bubble Boy

Fowzya Abdalrahman Alhomedan　　　Children
Little Niece

Erika Rossio Marcapura　　　　Travel
Rincones De San Antonio

Robert Drew Peterson　　　　Travel
Road To The Dragon

Lorena Orozco Martinez　　　　Children
Little Miss

Mark Dominic Stephany　　　　Travel
Kingdom Upon Castle

Donald Szymanski Nature
Yosemite Falls

Jennifer Lyman Nature
Venetian Way

Allana Lynne Jose Children
So Innocent

Bruce Wayne Fonnest Other
Putting Shirt At The Vietnam Wall

Sarah Elaine Deardurff Other
Summer Shading

Wes T. Shaw People
Linny

Jared Michael Beasley   Animals/Pets
Chloe's Tub

Jay Kennedy   Nature
After A Fall Rain

Laurie Ipsen   Nature
Reminiscence

Teresia Jana Buxar   Nature
Camping At Lake Fraser

Kristine Marie Vasquez   Nature
Northern Lights From My Bedroom

Drew Pierre Redmond   Other
Card Reaction

Samuel Lin Steele　　　　　　　　　　　Travel
A Thai Welcome

Allen J. Farnham　　　　　　　　　　　Travel
Twilight Magic

Nicholas Adam Sopczak　　　　　　　　Other
Rushing

Rossanna Praino　　　　　　　　　　Children
Angel

Molly Sara Robinson　　　　　　　　　Nature
Everlasting Log

Melvin Rodriguez　　　　　　　　　　Other
If You Were This Small . . .

Jaqueline Ibragimov　　　　　　　　Nature
Your Sweetness Flower

Edward Alan Billingham　　　　　Animals/Pets
Daisy's Pond

April Renee Williams　　　　　　　Nature
Riverwalk

Deloris Yankey　　　　　　　　　Nature
Serenity

Debbie Lynn Baker　　　　　　　Children
Good Spaghetti

Rita J. Marie　　　　　　　　　Nature
North Carolina Sea Storm

Dean S. Cool — Nature
Sunset

Meshel Lynn Adams — Nature
Mt. Fuji Sunrise

Maxine Masterfield Smith — Animals/Pets
Bad Hair Day

Virginia Bryan — Animals/Pets
Mystic Noel

Sylvana Tapia — People
Sweaty Shell

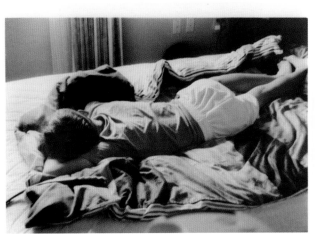

Katheleen Kang — Children
Youth

Ariel Elizabeth Waldman   Animals/Pets
Lucy

Orren Ford   Other
Sunset

Andrea Katherine Glass   Nature
Iced Over

Pamela Lynn Foglesong   Animals/Pets
Basket Case

Michelle A. Raposo   Travel
Je L'aime

Bridget K. Adam   Nature
Wonders Of Fall

130

Scott Allan Bieth   Travel
Above The Clouds

Annie Patton   Nature
Grasshopper

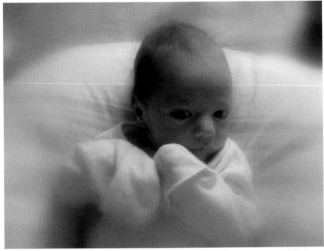

Yuliya Belenky   Children
Love Me

Pam June Grandmaison   Animals/Pets
Faith At Christmas

Sarah K. Brown   Children
All I Want For Christmas Is My Two Front Teeth

Kaylee R. Westcott   Nature
Lake Simcoe

Mallory Rae Lawrence   Portraiture
Illusive Freeway

Lisa Anne Esposito   Children
Classic Beauty

Keighla Marie Dalton   Travel
Eiffel Tower

Mark Reid Arnold   Action
Jump

Becky Taylor   Nature
Alive

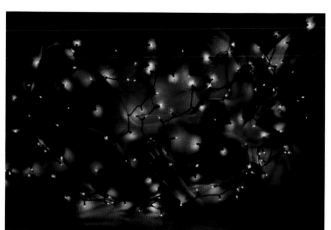

Justin Taylor   Portraiture
Illumination

Conrad Charels John Sullivan　　　　Animals/Pets
Winter Dog

Thomas W. Hart　　　　Nature
Rainbow

Jennifer L. Matzke　　　　Animals/Pets
Bunny

Chan Ong　　　　People
Deep Thoughts

William J. G. Reilly　　　　Nature
Afternoon Oar

Michael Allen Campa　　　　Other
The Spare Room

Danielle N. Mormino   Nature
Battery Park

Randall Jay Crews   People
Electric Guitar

Robyn Kindt   Nature
Mother And Baby

Ali Elizabeth Whittemore   People
Lonely Girl In A Diner

Randall Jay Crews   People
Late For School

Hajnalka Timea Lyons   Travel
Wales

Kelly L. Dean   Nature
Black Dog At Play

Traci L. Kimball   Children
In Thought

John Luke Hay   Nature
Untitled

Taylor Lynn Bean   Nature
Kookanusa At Night

Monica Jo Pyle   Nature
Spring In Bloom

Victoria Tabaracci   Portraiture
I Will Win

Antoinette Dawn Poor   Nature
Hello, There

Patricia Lynn McKinney   People
Mystic

Jennifer Nicole Avello   Portraiture
Drowning Out The World

Corrina Pam Hawkins   Nature
Great Australian Icon

Stacey Walker   Children
Travon

Kimberly D. Ryder   Children
Sweet Innocence

Tonya A. Gardner   Children
Prettiest Fairy Of All

Lisa Javaras McLaughlin   Other
Greek Church

Bianca Martinez   People
Me In The Snow

Gary Nelson   Animals/Pets
Shasta

Brad Jay Bearden   Portraiture
Erica

Laura L. Angus   Children
Innocent Love

Andreas Nickhorn   Nature
Explosion In The Sky

Gareth Smith   Animals/Pets
Eagle Owl

William Thomas Davis Sr.   Nature
Conimicut Light—Sundown

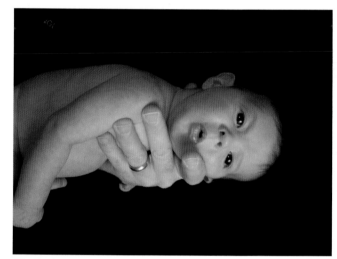

Kaylin Krystal Kennedy   Children
Cade

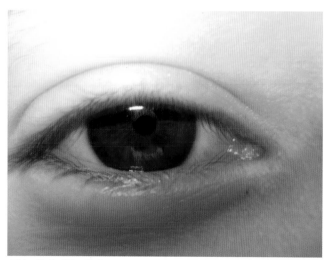

Abigail Ardiles Palmen   Other
Look At You

April Bush   Children
Pucker Up

Michael James Neubacher   Children
Curiosity

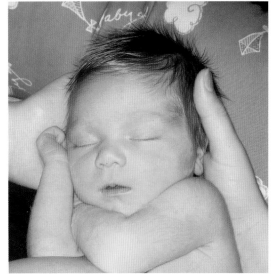

Katie Kay Phillips   Children
Aren't I Precious?

Carol J. Koyne   Animals/Pets
Dancing In The Park

Aaron Richard Nash   Children
Dress Up

Patricia Carol Clark   People
Great Moment

Bill D. Avery   Animals/Pets
Clean Leap

Emily Anne Martin People
Behind The Wheel

John P. Swarts Nature
Turkey Tracks

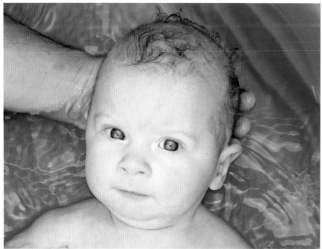

Michael Douglas Mabe Children
Pool Eyes

Jacqueline Dawn Newsome Nature
Peace In The Valley

Sherry Anne DeLauder Children
Caught You!

Jessica Dawn Harper Other
Abuse—You Don't Have To Go Through It Alone!

Matthew Crouch Travel
Arc De Triomphe

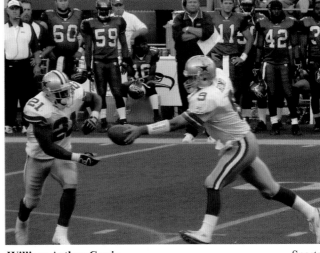

William Arthur Cowie Sports
The Hand-Off

Carla Mae Taylor Animals/Pets
Best Friend

Kristan Hope Micucci Children
Get In, Let's Go

Samantha Eileen McKown People
Surprise

Trey Campbell Nature
Awaiting The Fall

Rebecca Jane Brookes-Tsang   Nature
The Power Of The Earth

Stacie Lynn Fain   Travel
Alaska Beauty

Barbara L. McBride   Nature
Blazing Sunset

Katie Rose Ramaley   Nature
Sixteen Graves

Kayla Rae Christensen   Nature
The Nymph Fountain

Nickki L. Ayala   Nature
Summer Nostalgia

Deborah Ann Mooney   Animals/Pets
The Tongue

Bennie P. Jenkins   People
Oops, I Can See Your Wisdom Teeth

Timothy C. Krueger   Travel
Chicago Sunrise

Celsie I. Steinmetz   Nature
Barn

Mike Butler   Nature
Red Tree With Vine

Roseanne Bottone   Travel
Wild Blue Yonder

Alice Marie Stidman　　　　　　　　　Children
Grandma's Garden In Full Bloom

Annissa Dianne Boc　　　　　　　　　Other
Memories Of Summer Camp

Josh Moto　　　　　　　　　Nature
Blessings

Kayla Raye Johnson　　　　　　　　　Travel
Through The Trees

Alyse Nichole Gandalone　　　　　　　　　Animals/Pets
I Always Knew I'd Find You, Even Before We Met

Megan Leigh Eanes　　　　　　　　　Nature
Swing

Ida N. Gorman   Other
A Cascading Ascent On The Steps Of Time

Loressa Anita Clisby   Travel
Gondolas

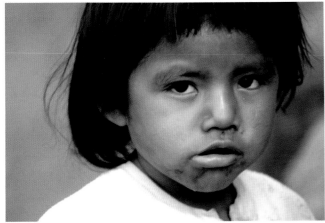

Michael Lee Mazo   Children
Hope

Cyndi Ann Kearse   People
Funny Faces

Kimberly A. Owens   Children
My Angel Face

Cornellia Kate Miller   Nature
Nature's Cathedral

Kylee Lynn O'Dwyer Nature
Sunset In Noosa

Nicole Robin McClure Animals/Pets
Brave Heart

Chris Thomas Turck Nature
Thought

Susan D. Jackson Animals/Pets
Bull"Dozer"

Elizabeth Robin Barr Animals/Pets
Last Morning At The Cottage

Sara Louise Van Arkel Nature
The Credit River

Kelsie Ann Hendricks   Other
The Front Line

Erika C. Selisky   Nature
Okinawan Cave

Tara Savina Vassallo   Animals/Pets
Buckwheat

Sarah Prichard   People
Baby Cow

Cary Kozak   Other
Red Wash Out

John Peter Nemarich   Nature
Mountain Stream

Vicky Jo Davis   Nature
Blazing Sky

Tabatha Ann Gregersen   Other
Girls And Ghost Train

Kaitlyn Davis Moeller   Portraiture
Stop The Separation

Daniel Samuel Lichtenstein   Other
New York Taxi

Dani Joyce   Nature
Sunset

Sara Lee Burden   Nature
Elk Falls

Georgia Kay Hughes   Nature
Rock On, Rainbow!

Meredith Ellen Barnes   Travel
London Eye

Amy Mae Nicholson   People
Focused Glance

Katie A. Carey   Travel
Wood

Hannah Rebekah Kent   Nature
Dry Shadows

Krista Ann Hamilton   Children
Mud Shirt

Michelle C. McCann   Children
Lil' Miss Attitude

Alex Daniel Ognjenovski   Sports
Burleigh Point

Rodney Howard Thill   Travel
Walking Tall

Isabel Gagne   Children
Liam

Erica Noelle Duncan   Nature
Jardin Majorelle

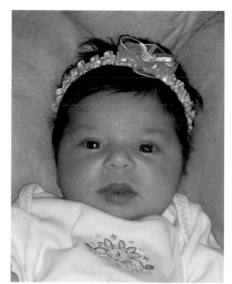

Elena Mendelevich   Children
I'm Cute!

Ron L. Profitt   Animals/Pets
Spoiled Dog

Cory Chaffee   Children
Peek-A-Boo

Kelley Kossan   People
Minnesota Fisherman

Sharon L. Mahoney   Children
I Love Eggs

Ari Adam Segal   Portraiture
Untitled

Natalia Segal   Portraiture
Hila

James Douglas Nicoll Travel
Vatican

Steven Lynn Moore Humor
Got Milk?

Mary Jo McCombs Animals/Pets
Posing Ducks

Mallory Jean Agard People
New Orleans Street Artist

Alexis Briana Calhoun People
Swoosh

Toni Ann Foley Other
I Love To Smile

Tera Marie Van Herk   Nature
Dominican Republic

Misty Williams   Children
Heaven's Angel

Cheryl Alice Sawchenko   Nature
A Lone Little Tree

Caitlyn Rebecca Irvin   Other
Contents Of My Purse

Claire Gay Daniels   Animals/Pets
Sisterly Love

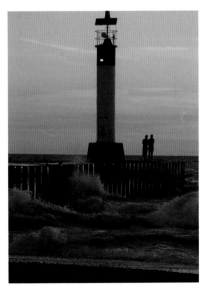

Mark L. Henkell   Other
Night Walk

153

Tanya Grausam   Nature
Sunshine Over The Barossa Valley

Khadijah Gethers   Humor
Fun Time

Maddie Alexandra Hanlon   Other
Creighton

Celena Johnson   People
Hands Of Time

Shannon Paterson   Animals/Pets
Cool Moose

Judy Nicole Horst   Other
The Green Rope

Nicholas Johnathan Cook   Other
When Not In Use

Leelah Dawn Dill   Children
All Cleaned Up

Lindsay Susan Dunlop   Nature
Favorite Place In The World

Don Roy Johnson   Travel
West Highland Way

Brailyn Tyrell Johnsgaard   Nature
Saskatchewan Sunset

Shelbi D. Clemens   Children
My Little Cowboy

Willie McNeal   Nature
Faces In The Mountains

Mike James Monaghan   Nature
The Bee And The Sun

Jon Holloway   People
A Daddy's Euphoria

John Cornelius Versnel IV   Nature
The Red House In Winter

Wesley Adam Karn   Travel
Fraser Island

Richard Peter Parnell   Animals/Pets
Coming In For Landing

Juan Gerber   Nature
Straddle Sunset

Jerry Scott Marang   Nature
Mary's Favorite

Simon Parnell Burns   Animals/Pets
Incandescent Stare

Joyce Malynda Rollins   Animals/Pets
What's For Supper?

Jacqueline Anne Peebles   Animals/Pets
Baby Doll

Rachel Tipton   Animals/Pets
Memories Of Sampson

Francis Paul Bertrand Travel
Sydney Nightscape

Abbie Lyn Helgerson Children
Saying Goodbye

Patricia Ann Yakowicz Nature
Saddle River Winter

Tracey Lynnette Wilson Children
First Birthday At The Pool

Rachel Concetta Falgout Travel
Daibutsu

David Anthony Seck Children
Jared At The Zoo

Paul A. Somers   Nature
December Sunset

John Clifford Bass Sr.   People
Daddy Smiling

Suzanne Heidenheim   People
My Angels

Megan Marie Lewallen   Nature
The Falls

Rebecca Ann Jablonski   Nature
The Leap

Daniela Elizabeth Mason   Travel
Paris

Priscilla Patricia Sousa   People
True Emotion

Pat A. Serak   Nature
Winter Window

Nichole Marie Curtis   People
White Hat

Lashondra Thomas   People
My Girls

Paul Chris Kunkel   Nature
Colors Of Autumn

Felicia Lynn Tompkins   Action
No Diving

Jennifer Ann Miles　　　　　　　　　Children
Tranquility

Tonia Marie Ralph　　　　　　　　　Children
My Sister And I

Katie Marie Randall　　　　　　　　Humor
Christmas Excitement

Courtney M. Volk　　　　　　　　　Nature
One

Elie Sarraf　　　　　　　　　　　Travel
Long Way From Home

Jordan William Matchett　　　　　People
The Jazzman

Tracy L. Crabtree　　　　　　　　　　　Nature
Fall Leaves

Steve Foster　　　　　　　　　　　People
Half Dollar

Melissa Ann Lilley　　　　　　　　　　　Nature
Clouds And Water

David Eric Houle　　　　　　　　　　　Animals/Pets
King

Ally Marie Monheim　　　　　　　　　　　Sports
The Trenches

Marco Antonio Sanchez　　　　　　　　　　　People
Mexican Blue Eyes

Carol Merriam   Action
On This Ride

Holly Laurie Bromley   Nature
Storm

Alexandra Angelica Diana   Portraiture
Sometimes I Feel Attractive

Alicia Marie Jacobs   Travel
The Eiffel Tower In Paris, France

Joann Johnson   Nature
Ice Storm

Alexandria Jo Willging   Nature
Defying Physics

Chelsea T. Benoit　　　　　　　　　　Travel
Lady Liberty And Her City

Kumseok Jung　　　　　　　　　　Other
Steps

Charlotte Jane Arthur　　　　　　Animals/Pets
High Alert

Kelly Maire Baldwin　　　　　　Animals/Pets
Bunny Kisses

Emily Maureen Johnston　　　　　Animals/Pets
Whale

Godwine Lee　　　　　　　　　　Travel
City Of Light

Janet Myers   Children
Stevie's Trip

Whitney Rae Wilson   Action
I Flip

Cheryl Hodges Williams   Nature
Red Woods

Bobby Jean Yeoman   Children
Pleasant Distraction

Heather E. Jacimore   Other
Take Off

Adam Thomas Scott   Portraiture
The Swooning Woman

Mrs. Colby R. Young　　　　　Children
He Loves Me

Eugenie Marie Deon　　　　　Children
Our Little Santa

Diane N. Van Boxmeer　　　　Nature
Hibiscus

Ian Phares　　　　　Animals/Pets
Dog's Eye View

Perry J. Bonck　　　　　Nature
Self-Gratification

Lorrie Popow　　　　　Children
At Your Service

James Wyatt Long   Nature
Hills

Tyler Joe Snavely   Other
The Strength To Rebuild

Andrew Davis Pyle   Animals/Pets
The Bird's Stare

Judith Mary-Alice Furness   Nature
Under The Sun

Jenny Seager   Animals/Pets
Surf Chick!

Sherry Patterson   Animals/Pets
Standing Guard

Olivier Lavoie   Nature
Acropole Mount, Charlevoix

Julian Payne   Nature
Marsh

Beth Anthony   Travel
New Zealand 2006

Aga J. Zabron   Nature
At The Park

Cecille H. Kalafut   Travel
Without Ever Knowing The Way

Kayla Alexandra Lascasas   Nature
Lilac Love

Michael Feldstein   Nature
City Sunset

Anne Schaefer   Travel
Angkor Wonder

Toby Gifford Lywood   Nature
Sunrise Over Porlock

Brittany Webber   Animals/Pets
Maddie

Amanda Uskuraitis   Nature
Raindrops

Sandy Mueller   Nature
Easter In Texas

Annicia Marie McLellan   Nature
A Flower Abloom

Eva Martinez   Children
Mommy's Precious Little One

Josie Cougar Stewart   Animals/Pets
Millie

Dan James Stork   Travel
River City

Rachel Elizabeth Odom   Nature
Swimming Hole In Ocoee, Tennessee

Joanne Louise Tyo   Animals/Pets
Western

William LeRoy Cook　　　　　　　　　Children
Grandson And Bee-Bee

Stacey Thompson　　　　　　　　　Animals/Pets
D. J. Montellle

Patricia Ann Gerin　　　　　　　　　Animals/Pets
How Do I Look?

Les J. Kneeland　　　　　　　　　Portraiture
Still Standing Pretty

Kina L. Fafard　　　　　　　　　Children
My Little Troublemaker

Devon Montgomery Baines　　　　　　　People
Me And My Grandpa

Nina Price   People
Untitled

Charlotte Welch   Other
Reflections Of Light

Kenna R. Davidson   Animals/Pets
Megan's Hibiscus

Michelle Sukert   Nature
A Diamond In The Rough

Pamela D. Stidham   Children
Untitled

Caterina Buhoci   Animals/Pets
Rational Gaze

Yahsha Tamidah Mellen   Children
The Pose

Tuesday Ann Deon   Nature
The Hunter

Amanda Guajardo   Nature
Ducks

Rhiannon Jane Ziebell   Animals/Pets
A Horse's Fairytale

Heinz Riemer   People
Rainy Day On 5th Avenue

Tracy Darlene Holmes   Animals/Pets
Dank In A Tree

Douglas L. Smith   Nature
Sunrise After Storm

Elizabeth Greve   People
Eclipse Belly

William C. Griffin   Animals/Pets
Beauty Of Wildlife

Samantha Brittany Kidd   Nature
Wings Of Paradise

Sandra Michelle Gibney   Nature
View From Grouse

Sonia Rose D'Andrea   Nature
Waterlily

Brandy Marie Winkler Children
Tanner

Carole C. Vandeusen Animals/Pets
Christmas Bunnies

Rick Beland Nature
Light Fading

Kelsey M. Smith Nature
Burgundy Star

Jenetta J. Steed Nature
Bird Of Winter

Michelle Marie Castro Children
By The Lake

Scottye J. Cash   Animals/Pets
In The Eye Of The Beholder

Elsy Alicia Salgado   Children
Felicidad En Pobreza

Charissa Ann Calvelage   Nature
Sunrise In Maine

Bridget Dunn   Other
Untitled

Suwela Esteban   Animals/Pets
Happy Birthday April And Leilani

Meg Elizabeth Swallow   People
Venice Local With Pigeons

Rene Michelle Sabo   Nature
Untitled

Sandra Anderson   Animals/Pets
Donatella And Nobie

A. L. Nagy   Nature
Untitled

Joanne Stetter   Nature
Hunting Honey

Jessica Ann Boivin   People
Intrigue

Karoline Lopardo   Nature
A Modest Beauty

Steve Martin Johnston Nature
Start Of Day

Trish Costa Nature
Flower Beauty

Frederick Swafford Children
Julia Celeste

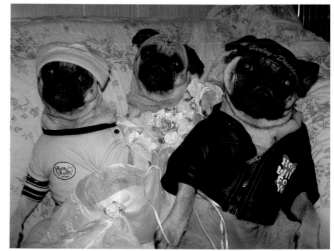

Brenda L. Fulk Animals/Pets
Our Beautiful Girls

Jeff Lyles Nature
Bear Cub

Jo-Anne Mary McLaren Nature
Summer Beauty

Diane D'amours   Nature
Watch Out!

Carrie Rose Croshier   Nature
Sun In Darkness

Shelby Erin Neace   Children
Baby Love

Denise Sawyer   Animals/Pets
Hobie's First Christmas

Lindsay Rae Turnbull   People
Timeless

Ilonka Lelkes   Nature
In The Shade

Heather Lynn Fillman — Nature
Pollination!

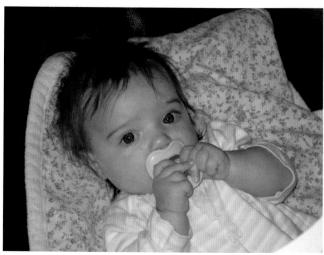

Rhonda Patrice Yankey — Children
Sarah

Joseph M. Morales — Nature
South Padre Island Sky

Blake Lee Reid — Nature
The Creek

Sam Mayel-Afshar — Portraiture
Gabriela X

Paul Bradford Gardner — Sports
Jalama Beach Sunset

Iliana G. Deltcheva   Nature
Untitled

Shenelle Rose Archibald   Animals/Pets
Pure Innocence

Jenna Layne Schell   Children
Hmong Village Children

Meghan Springer   Nature
Sun's Vision

Nadia Cotter   Nature
Orchidology

Belinda Jane Johansen   Children
Peaceful

Louise Hayes Nature
Bird Of Paradise

Lauren Elizabeth Colton Animals/Pets
Shelter

Jennifer Lynn Bigby Nature
Calm Day

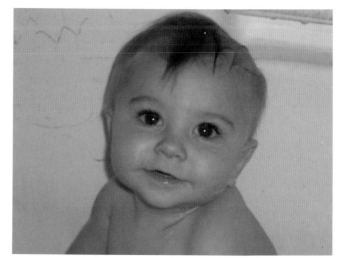

Holly Rene Keever Children
My Lil' Turtle Head!

Cristin Arel Nature
Amsterdam

Theresa E. Litourneau Animals/Pets
Stella

Rosemarie Ann Gerard　　　　　　　　　Nature
Autumn Rainbow

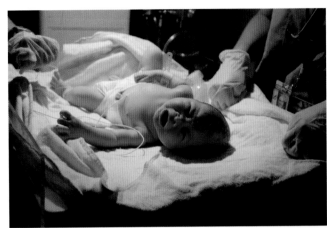

Paul Kongkham　　　　　　　　　Children
Happy Birthday

Judy Broscious　　　　　　　　　Nature
Longwood—She Ladies

Lynda Bernardi-Wray　　　　　　　　　Children
Ethan

Maria Paula De Virgilio　　　　　　　　　Nature
Blackcomb Glacier

John Arthur Randall　　　　　　　　　Nature
Cultus Lake

Amber Nicholson   Nature
The Elephant

Sandra Coe   Humor
Brittnay Who?

Lisa M. Van   Animals/Pets
Snow Dogs Staying Dry

Pamela Ann Gray-Faude   Nature
Christmas Sunset 2007

Danyell A. Dilk   Animals/Pets
I'm Free

Robin L. Towe   Children
Quiet Time

Susie Thompson   Nature
In Awe Of The Ocean

Iris E. Santiago   Animals/Pets
Lucky In The Sun

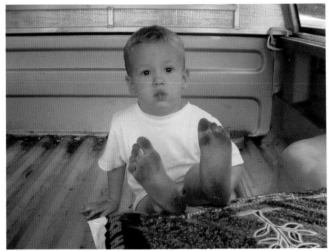

Guy Ann Sheffield   Children
Dirty Feet

Mark C. Bruce   Animals/Pets
Shakin' It!

Mechelle M. Samuel   Children
Christmas

Karen F. Wright   Children
Flower Girl Moment

Stacie Elizabeth Hurley   Other
Gledhill

Kathie Yant   People
Little Girl Dreaming

Erica L. Oramas   Nature
Winter Wonderland

Jackie Yvonne Blakeley   Animals/Pets
Longing

Lisa Plourde   Travel
Grand Falls, Canada

Samantha Cunningham   Nature
Tiger Lilies

Lawrence Lauro   Animals/Pets
Waiting For Christmas

Tami A. Joca   Animals/Pets
Cute Little Puppy

Kristi Jean Nelson   Children
Untitled

Ryan Harrison Johnson   Other
My Hobby

Lee Gordon Christoffersen   Nature
Mountain Sunset

Earl Victor Dunnington Jr.   Portraiture
Apache Rain Dancer

Andrea Palafox   Travel
The Man And The Mosque

Bonny P. Teynor   Portraiture
Joy Of Life

Kenneth E. Nelson   Nature
Into The Sunset

Sally Ann Orm   Children
Sarah Mae

Lynn Hill   Other
Rainbow Over Keene

Patrick Lacroix   Nature
Green Nature

Jason Boling People
Sweet Sorrow In Bratislava

Janet A. Strickland Animals/Pets
Smile And The World Smiles With You

Jonathan Robert Robinson Other
Power

Candace Lee Ganje Nature
Friends In Winter

Joannah Angelene, Dinah Matheson Nature
Quiet Surroundings

Caitlin Shay Bullock Nature
Tired And Uninspired

Tabitha Jayne Ritchie   Travel
Sunrise At The Beach

Suzette Marie Esneault   Children
Sisterly Love

Nona Jean Taylor   Travel
Place Of Peace And Quiet

Shay Thomas   Children
Faith Thomas

Jo Anne Mielke   Animals/Pets
The Amazing Sam Siam!

Mary Margaret Brower   Children
The Touch Of Nature

Mel Dorman   Nature
Summer Fun

Dawn M. Sharples   Children
My Little Model

Lisa Lynn Docherty   Nature
Evening Sky

Tracey Alice Mabe   Nature
Daylily

A. J. Brown   Animals/Pets
Cat Jumping Down

Jenna Rae Witherow   Nature
First Winter's Lick

Cindy B. Garvin
Children
Bathtime

Daniel Scott Clem
Travel
Nightlife

Anna Rebekah Franz
Animals/Pets
My Dog, Molly

Shirley Louise Calvert
Action
Happy Appy

Kimberly Ann Wood
Children
Baby Wyatt

Jessica Rose Hokaszewski
Nature
Calm Simplicity

Kim Karikis Children
Billy Bear

Donna Marie Novak Animals/Pets
Chloe

John Kelly Animals/Pets
We Can All Be Friends, In Spite Of Our Differences

Thomas Pinkerton Children
Freedom

Oscar Marczynski Animals/Pets
Greek Tortoise

Bradford James Powell Children
Should I?

Jacob R. Lefferts III   People
Blonde On My Beach

Donald J. McLain   Children
Say Cheese

John Edward Maas   Nature
Spring Into Summer

Barbara Hale Edgington   Animals/Pets
Taking It All In

David A. Warren   Children
Anya, The Mouth

Heather Hobbs Wiley   Animals/Pets
Oscar In The Flowers

Lindsay L. Berndt   Animals/Pets
Excuse Me!

Kristin Claire Tangel   Animals/Pets
Fly With The Moon On Their Wings

Caitlan Elizabeth Mascolo   Nature
Change

Sherron Swapp Jensen   Humor
Cheeky Boy

Tom Jenkins   Other
Three Bears Cafe

Tara Lyn Sutherland   People
Little Tiger

195

Christian K. Fridrich   Children
Ahhh . . .

Arthur Gene Propps Jr.   Animals/Pets
Puppy Kisses—Annie And Floyd

Liz Jordan   Children
It's Santa

Matthew Daniel Gillis   Nature
Fern Stream

Rita Antoinette Pease   Portraiture
Conifer Colorado

Susan Caro   Humor
Mmm . . . Yummy!

196

William A. Gresens   Other
Sunset At Darwin

Aaron J. Dumford   Sports
Ghost Rider

Connie S. Bush   Children
Praying For Fish!

Shane Gorski   Travel
Lake At Lugano

Noelle Kowalick   Children
Buzz Cuts

Christian McClelland Reid   Other
Bridge

Jennifer Lynn Zanzig   Nature
Reach To The Sky

Kristin Suzanne Hays   Nature
Frozen Leaf

Jennifer Lane Dunevant   Animals/Pets
At Attention

Kylie McPherson   Nature
Sunset

Michelle Maree Laruccia   Animals/Pets
Hippo Symmetry

Donita Cogburn   Nature
Heaven Is Open

Linda Strawser   Nature
Frozen In Time

Valerie Renee Rice   People
Joyous Exit

Chris Ward   Humor
Grace Meets Tigger!

Sharon Lynn Kelley   Nature
Ruby Tuesday

Christa Boyer   Nature
Autumn Beauty

Consuelo M. Flores   Children
Nicky

Janessa Ochoa   Travel
Window To The Skies

Jenny Lynn Heintz   Nature
The Little Things

John Joseph Trombino   Nature
Taking The Sun

Eleanor Caroline Cacioppo   Animals/Pets
Mommy And Me

Arthur Christopher Lloyd   Nature
Solo Point

Edward Hampton Shelander   Nature
Glory After Sunset

Maurice Fred Geraud Animals/Pets
My Dog, Jacques

Kimberly Marie Jilks Children
Joshua Hayden

Patty A. Woodyard Animals/Pets
Hawk

Carole Elizabeth White Animals/Pets
Purrrfect

Jessica Lynn Hurd People
Canvas Hands

Mike Ly Children
Baby Cool

Caroline Rose Orlando People
Wedding Flower Girl

Caitlin Saville Other
Bell Tower

Laura Susan McCarthy Travel
Sail Away

Susan Joy Thom People
Precious

Martin John Robert Treaster People
Courtney

Samuel Christopher Taylor Other
Beautiful

Josh James Udall Nature
The Hills

Kane Matthew Silbereisen Travel
Jungle Train

Constantine Leoussis Itkowitz Nature
Bird In Central Park

Ruth Ann Craig Children
October Beach

Warren Nederpelt People
Fire

Barbara Jean Lovejoy-Welch Children
My Three Sons

203

Anna Nadine Chalmers Nature
Birkalla

Desirae Lynn Ankney Nature
Happiness

Jean Valtierra Animals/Pets
Gatekeeper

Lucy Anna Walton Children
Cheeky Chaps!

John A. Daley Animals/Pets
Naptime

Samantha Vivian West Other
Our First Fire

Donna Gaudet   Nature
Walk In Peace

Tara-Lynn Disher   Travel
Under The Arches

June Rader Cooper   Nature
Mama's Farm

Crystal Alvina-Lee Wrixon   Nature
Midnight Sun

Kirsten Michela Manville   People
Reflections

BeLinda Lee Pickelsimer   Children
Reflections

Harry Robert James Gemmell　　　　　Other
Chain-Linked

Adam W. Mohl　　　　　Other
One-Way Passage

Bonnie F. Sallet　　　　　Animals/Pets
Praying Mantis

Jeff W. Boyer　　　　　People
My Grandson

Mary Alice Newman　　　　　Other
Reflection

Elaine E. Hankin　　　　　Nature
Quiet Time

Danielle Tremblay   Animals/Pets
The Real Santa Claus

Victoria Lynn Coy-Stout   Nature
Before The Storm

Karen T. Sharkey   Nature
Verga '99

James Eugene O'Connell   Nature
Sunrise At Ballygally, Ireland

Kenzie Mortensen   Children
Looking Back

Jennifer K. Marris-Walker   Animals/Pets
King Of The Hill

Frederick Marshall   Other
Flowers Created By My Wife

Jennifer Nicole Hartman   Nature
Sunset In The Amazon

Bill Delaney   Animals/Pets
Shania—Country Cat

Farid Mehrzad   People
Old, Tired, Poor Man In Afghanistan

Amanda Leigh Law   Children
Albertan Baby

Stacey Elaine Orr   Children
Kaitlynn In The Fall

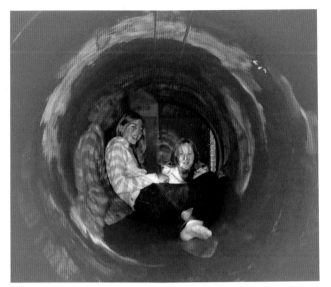

Glenn Albert Gamotis　　　　　　　　Children
Young Ladies In Red

Kelsey Marie Steinmetz　　　　　　Animals/Pets
Focusing

Dee D. Mitchell　　　　　　　　Animals/Pets
Who Is Watching Who

William George White　　　　　　　Travel
A Trip To Paradise

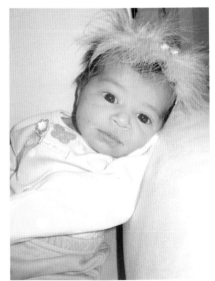

Chloé Collette Santangelo　　　　　Children
Baby Bella

Audra Marie Studebaker　　　　　　Nature
The Summer's Last Sunset

Valentina Vivianiová   Sports
Wrestling Game

Anita B. Venkataramana   Nature
Nature's Amphitheater

Doug Eicher   Animals/Pets
Golden Finch

Paula Terese Ivanoskos   Nature
Serenity

Dorothy N. Merritt   Nature
Birds

Sonia Rosario   Children
Jayvin

210

Barbara Izzard   Nature
Serenity

Tom C. Marsh   Nature
Winter

Jimmy Dawson   Nature
Outdoor Critters

Janet Lynn Souther   Nature
Lone Crane

Savannah Victoria Todd   Nature
River View

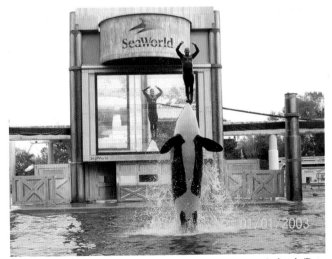

Darrin Lemons   Animals/Pets
Flying High

Harry Troise Lyles   Travel
Bike Rack

Kayla Dawn Wesley   Animals/Pets
Got It!

Debra Hoekenga   Sports
Got Air?

Ricardo Vasquez   Other
The White House From Jefferson's Eyes

Jody Lynn Vandellen   Animals/Pets
Our Princess, Susie

Janell Lynn Poenitske   Animals/Pets
Boy, You're Tall!

Louise Roy   Nature
Arboretum

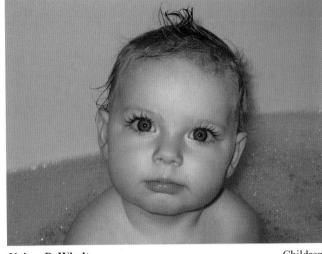

Krissy DeWindt   Children
Hannah Bernice Evans

Peter Koster   Nature
Fall

David W. Wilson   Nature
Out Of Many, One Beautiful Flower

Kurt R. Weber   Animals/Pets
Stinky

Arianna Renee Paratchek   Animals/Pets
Three Is Too Crowded

Lindsey Marie Morgan Nature
The Sky Is The Limit

Haley Buller Nature
Aloha

Jessica Luong Nature
The Beautiful Aspects Of Life

Curt James Brooks Travel
Denali—The Great One

Tim D. Richardson Nature
Our Glory

David Porter Sports
A Perfect Moment

Jennifer S. Spears Nature
Peace

Elizabeth S. Kyle Children
My Big Brother

Courtney Marie Johnson Animals/Pets
Dashing Through The Snow

Bridget Ann Sylva Children
Where Are The Pumpkins?

Zane R. Frakes Animals/Pets
My Lab, Rock

Rio M. Gache Other
Pews

Marty Pickering Animals/Pets
Miss Kitty

Carissa Nicole Read Travel
Innocence In Mexico

Brandi Lei Smith Children
Having A Ball

Dee Sonera People
High School Musical Fans

Sandra L. Adams Children
Shaun The Fireman

Michelle Renea Watson Other
Christmas Joy

Dion L. Kohler Sr.   People
The Spirit Of Christmas

DeLacey Amber Limbaugh   People
Eye

Yvette Belcher   Animals/Pets
Shall We Dance?

Deborah A. Kruse   Nature
October Sunrise

William L. Oshier   Animals/Pets
Missed Friend

Stephh Gloria Pattison   Nature
Sunny

Carma J. Robinson Nature
Peek-A-Boo

Jessica Paige Desjean Children
Baby Blues

Samantha R. Semones Portraiture
If You Could Only See

April A. Hauser Nature
Rainbow On Lake Michigan

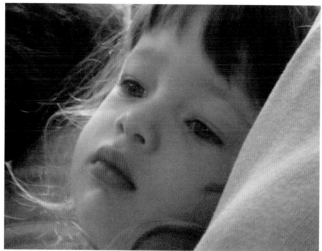

Marcel Daia Children
Natural Beauty

Sheridan Hastings Beesley Nature
Frosted Barbed Wire

Farhana S. Choudhury Nature
Birds Watching Sunset

Theresa Ryan Nature
Clouds Dancing At Sunset

Linda L. Brant Travel
Aletha Winters

Michelle Loren Children
Waking Autumn

Natalie Anne Spencer Animals/Pets
Cleaning

Deborah Wilkinson Nature
Daisy

Dana Marie Cottone People
To Dance Freely Is To Enjoy Life

Timothy James Cullen Nature
The Beauty Of The Monarch

Valerie Jean Hart Children
Smiles With Daddy

Roseanne Dedona Nature
Canadian Sky

Tammy Boyd Animals/Pets
Shaggy, Close-Up

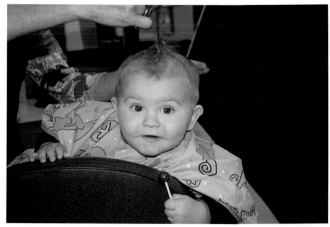

Dawn Strobel Children
Haircut

Megan Renae Walker   Action
Spotlight

Elizabeth Jo Franck   Animals/Pets
McDonald's

Rachael Nicole Stone   Children
Blessed Are The Children

Tierra Noelle Guzman   Nature
Ocean Rays

Deb J. Edgett   Nature
Day's End

Megan Lynn Farley   Travel
The Fog

Kearstin Rew   Nature
Taken Flight

Jacqueline O'Shea Taylor   Animals/Pets
Heaven

Wayanne Mae Kruger   People
Morning Beauty

Tarryn Shea McCollum   Portraiture
Love

Heather D. Exarhos   Children
Peaceful Slumber

Laura Elizabeth Daly   People
Shadow Person

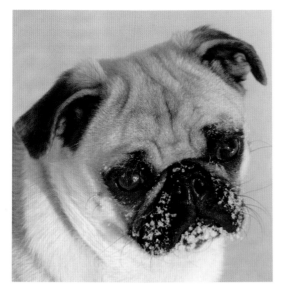

Charlotte A. Francoeur   Animals/Pets
Peanut

Eric Anthony Brucia   Other
On The Brink Of Eternity

Lis Engel   Other
Rhythms

Demetrius M. Williams   Nature
The Grand Canyon

Katie M. Braunlin-Stites   Animals/Pets
Curious Fawn

Judith Nilsa Batista   Travel
Caribbean Sunset

Katherine Ann Hamersly   People
Isabella

Carole A. Miller   Animals/Pets
Aren't I Cute?

Theresa Ann Sammartino   Children
Playful

Charles Wayne Baltz   Nature
Northshore Reef

Bruce E. Spencer   Animals/Pets
Gizmo

Rachel Elizabeth Terrana   People
Into The Sun

Debi J. Kiniry　　　　　　　　　　Nature
Pennsylvania Path

Sasha Majerovsky　　　　　　　Portraiture
Christmas In New York

Tracy Marie Terrill　　　　　　　Children
The Devil In My Child

Hamie C. Hersom　　　　　　　　Nature
Tangled

Eric Poulin　　　　　　　　　　　Nature
Life On A Blade Of Grass

Dennis Patrick Martin　　　　　　Nature
Mandarin Duck

Sarah Eve Leahy　　　　　　　　　　Children
Me And Twinkle

Marty Uhl　　　　　　　　　　Nature
Sunset

Manda Celeste Schall　　　　　　　　People
Pace Yourself

Jennifer Khan　　　　　　　　　　Children
Sweet Memories

Ashley Elizabeth Evans　　　　　　　People
Friends Forever

Ashley Marie Bumgardner　　　　　　Nature
Summertime Blues

Julie Anne Jordan   Nature
The Last Green

Erica Ashby   People
The Leap

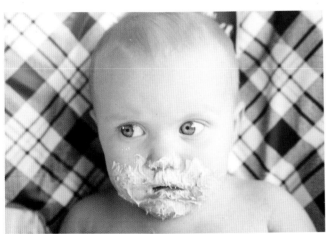

Nechola Antoinette King   Humor
Oh, Man, Please Gimme My Cake Back

Laura E. D'Orazio   Children
Love

Paul John Fisher   Nature
Springboro Road

Wendy L. Crimmins   Children
Where's My Pony?

Destiny L. Mills   People
The End Of A Summer Day

Fatima Alvinez Nacaytuna   Nature
Winter At The Lake

Gabrielle Blair Neavin   Nature
Busy Bee

Claire Ceravino   Nature
Bermuda Dreams

Eric Wayne Stewart   Nature
Mountain Waterfall

David Gordon Snow   Nature
Three Sisters

Allison Margaret Michael   Children
Evie At The Park

Benjamin Stephen Miller   Children
First Christmas

Amy Jill Garcia   Action
Kites

Alexis Nicole Moody   Nature
Beauty In Black And White

Amanda Jane Koprivech   Nature
Unchartered Path

John M.Capparelli   Animals/Pets
Mimi, Under The Covers

Whitney P. Mannes   Other
Summer Bliss

Linda Dian Lorenz   Animals/Pets
Friends

Eva R. Tumiel-Kozak   Animals/Pets
Without Me, No Way!

Angela M. Ray   Nature
Beauty

Kristen R. Stewart   Children
Nissan Girl

Deborah Ann Montgomery   Animals/Pets
The Black Swan

Adrienne Florence Snyder   Nature
Sun Shining Through On Charleston

Crystal Joy Lazore   Nature
Skyline

Herbert D. West   Nature
I See You

Lawrence David Christy   Children
Say Again

Kevin Peragine   Animals/Pets
Home Again

Teri Sherrell   Nature
Sunset In The Smokies

Aleena Farah Ahmed   Children
Cutie

Kayla Dawn Falsetti   Nature
The Small Things

Bernadette M. Atterberry   Nature
A Bug's Life

Krista S. Flinn   Travel
Mountains

Marlene E. Moore   Travel
The Blue Mosque

Melissa May Rogers   Travel
Polynesian View

Joy Marie Renfro   Animals/Pets
Which One Is Real?

Sara Katherine Wolf   Nature
Lilac

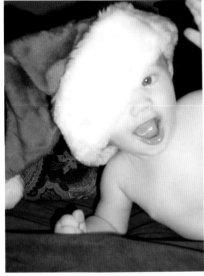

Christina Michelle Teague   Children
Little Santa

Dillon John Ezerins   Nature
Fraser Island Sunrise

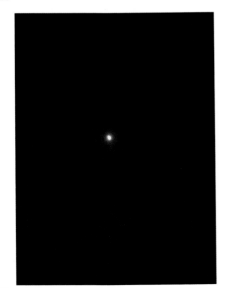

Lori G. Shunk   Nature
Nighttime

Liana Ivaylova Zhecheva   Other
Sun Cloning

Mauricio Quiroga   Nature
Everglades, Morning Fog

Jaymie Collette   Animals/Pets
Christmas Dogs

Anne Mills Brown   Travel
A New Day

Erica Lynn Coers   Nature
Yellow Hibiscus

Diane Messer   Children
Pucker Up

Darleen Leal   Animals/Pets
Hey There!

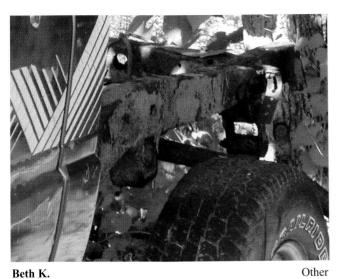

Beth K. Other
Axle

Stacey Leana Vaughn People
Time Out

Zee Loraine Miller Animals/Pets
Biker Babe

Jerico Rochelle Gould-May Animals/Pets
Duck

Angela Marie DiPalma Nature
Love Birds

Richard Freed Travel
Into The Deep

Shaun Milner   Nature
Keep The Home Fires Burning

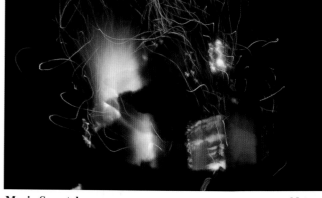

Maria Sawatzky   Nature
Campfire Sparks

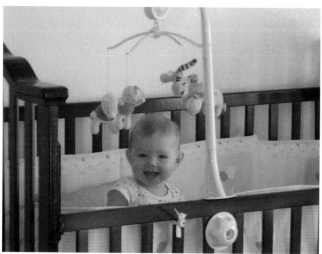

Josh P. Miller   Children
Breanna Waking Up From Nap

Melissa Ann Pasquariello   Other
Stonetown Bridge

Jenny Munro   Nature
Urbane River

Marvin E. Johnson   Animals/Pets
Cat Using Bathroom

236

Shannan Kelly   Children
Daddy And Me

Mariana Saieva   People
You're Cool If You Skate

Karen E. Meeks-El   Animals/Pets
The Wonders Of Nature

Elizabeth S. McDonald   People
Cowboy's Hard Day

Martine Ann Cook   Children
Bright Eyes

Brenda Kay Jones   Other
Love

James Paul Roper
Christmas Puppies
Animals/Pets

Lisa Marie Sanders
Palatka Berries
Nature

Abigail Marie Long
Toledo, Spain
Travel

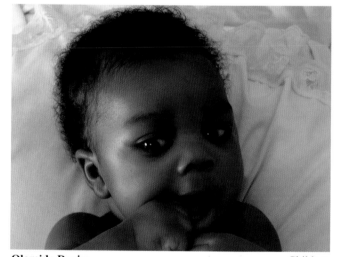

Olamide Davies
Better Than A Pacifier
Children

Danielle L. Moore
After The Storm
Nature

Lupe A. Sanchez
Santa's Helper
Animals/Pets

238

Joe Winters Children
New Beginning

Sharon Juanita Delesbore People
Boy To Man

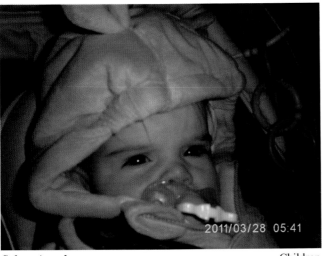

Salma Angulo Children
Hannah At Dusk

Laurie Anne McKinney Children
Huckleberry Mak

David Edward Underwood Nature
Peace

Christina Love Watson Children
Reflections

Sheryl L. Barker　　　　　　　　　　Children
World's Cutest Baby—Braden Farrell

Kimberly Marie Hurrle　　　　　　　Sports
Royals

Dori Allen　　　　　　　　　　　Animals/Pets
Shake It Off

Autumn Mariya Arnett　　　　　　Children
You're So Funny

Alexandra Simone Murphy　　　　　Nature
We Travel In Packs

Angelia D. Robinette-Dublin　　　Animals/Pets
Enjoying The First Snow

Laurena Pollock   Nature
Faces Of The Falls

Misty Marie Neltner   Travel
Hawaiian Tropics

Richard M. Kuehn   Nature
Christmas At The Ocean

Alex Herrera   Nature
Dandelion

John Rollie Crary   Nature
Pine Grove Snowstorm

Bradley Derring McCoy   Nature
Golden Sun

Megan Ransome   Animals/Pets
Droplet Of Water On Nose

Max D. Stokes   Portraiture
Broken Wagon Wheel

Olga Maria Colon   Children
My Son And Daughter

Parker D. Susong   Travel
Freedom's Will

Corissa Michelle Utter   People
My Son

Zara Ellen Courns   Children
Ryland

Adrianna Renae Parrott   Children
Untitled

Christopher Ryan DeHaven   Nature
Ageless Sunset

Dezerae Dawn Snow   Animals/Pets
Kitten In The Window

Emily Elizabeth Chastain   Nature
Swan

Sam Burke Winslow   Nature
Rhododendron

Loyce Leslie Green   Nature
Winterland

Kitti Puskas Action
Fast And Furious

Keely Tateossian Children
Ice Cream

Jackie Joyce Sorensen Nature
Winter Bench

Cheyenne A. Kling Other
Winter

Lisa Rena' Martin Animals/Pets
Have A "Dog-Gone" Merry Christmas

Dillon James Wray Other
Double Fire

Andrew Foderaro   Nature
Reflection

Jaime Sue Gallaway   Children
Day At The Races

Jamie Elizabeth Johnson   Animals/Pets
Awaiting Prey

Julie Sansom   Animals/Pets
My Naughty Dingoes Chewed Up My Feather Duster

Natan Wettstein   Nature
Wet Branch

Beth Weigel   Animals/Pets
Baleigh And Molly—First Snow

Channing Brianne Finch   Nature
High School Sunset

Omar Fernando Sanchez   Travel
Villa De Leyva

Savannah Tinsley Crawford   Other
My View Of Downtown

Jennifer Rebecka Fleck   Children
Chocolates And Bows

Jamie Nicholas Seymour   Nature
The Chase

Candee M. Homer   Children
All Hats Are Not Treated Equal

Barbara Ann Harmon   Other
River Of No Return

Christina M. Fairchild   Nature
Winter In The Park

Liliana Bustos   Animals/Pets
Ordinary Or Extraordinary?

Sue Smith   Nature
God's Glorious Beauty

Stephanie Anne Sullivan   Portraiture
Honesty

Joelle Ann Hedgspeth   Nature
Cherry Parfait

ARTISTS' PROFILES

AIELLO, LESLIE

This is a photo of my beautiful baby niece, Olivia. She is the youngest daughter to my sister, Stephanie. It was a sunny summer day, playing out in the yard. I sat her down in the grass as I watched her gaze onto her sister, Elena, swinging away on her swingset. That's why I named it "Thoughts," wondering what this little baby girl was thinking. I was in awe of her and I knew this was a winner! I have always enjoyed the expressions of children. You only have one chance to capture that perfect moment in time!

ALHOMEDAN, FOWZYA ABDALRAHMAN

I always wonder at how small my little niece, Aram Alsently, is. I call her "Nonah," which means "very little," in the Arab language. I love her a lot.

ALLEN, DORI

This is a picture of my dog, Riley. Not only he is my dog, he is my best friend. Every year after my hometown closes the swimming pool for the season, they let us bring our dogs to swim in the pool before draining it. Riley jumps in with reckless abandon and will swim for hours. Occasionally he will try to retrieve the safety buoys. He has not been successful at this yet, but I think he will keep trying until he is.

ANDRAHOVITCH, CARLY ANNA

My camera is always with me as I like to capture random beauty in nature. I get a visual not only in my mind, but preserved through a photo. This photo was taken as my boyfriend was setting up to go hunting. Camera handy, I imagined as if I were climbing the ladder. To show the stillness of my surroundings, I chose a black-and-white theme.

ANGUS, LAURA L.

I was playing with my grandson in his other grandmother's backyard when I realized I should be capturing these moments on camera. He stopped playing long enough to kiss a little wooden bird. When I downloaded the photo, I noticed the sun had implanted angel wings on his back. It was perfect, just like him.

ANTHONY, BETH

This photo was taken on a walk while visiting the thermal pools in Taopo, New Zealand. It's kind of a once-in-a-lifetime shot. It was my dream to visit New Zealand since I was a child and had the opportunity to go in March of 2005. I currently reside in Fort McMurray, Alberta. In my spare time I enjoy spending time with my family. I also enjoy reading, photography, Facebooking, and playing Phase Ten with family and any friends who I can sucker into playing.

ARCHIBALD, SHENELLE ROSE

I am an amateur photographer who has always had a love of photography. I have recently started my own business, Shenelle Rose Photography, and I'm hoping to gain more recognition. This photo was taken after much perseverance. My boyfriend, John, and I spent an entire afternoon in his backyard trying to get the perfect shot. I thought this one was beautiful.

ARMSTRONG, SUSAN GAYLE

They say a picture is worth a thousand words. This is our daughter Kim's priceless, nineteen-year-old cat named Peaches. We do this in her honor because of the love and joy she brings to us. May the peace and serenity of this inspire all who view her photo. I take many pictures, but once in a while a special one comes along.

ARNOLD, MARK REID

Matt, Joe, and Tom Arnold take to the air, briefly. The three brothers launched themselves into "The Ol' Swimmin' Hole" many times those summers we lived near this area. Going to the beach was about all we could afford while I was in grade school, but we made the most of it! One day, their mother and I paddled our old canoe out to where I could take this shot. "We were a lot closer than this looks," she says. "I thought they were going to land on me."

ARTURO, JULIE MARIE

Ever since my sophomore photography class, I have been in love with capturing moments through photographs. After my high school graduation, a bunch of my friends and I went to the beach for a week. The day after a large storm, my friend, Grace, and I decided to go for a walk on the beach to collect some shells. On the way out the door, I grabbed my friend's camera for fun. Once on the beach, Grace started grabbing little crabs that were running around. I was amazed at her ability to catch these fast little creatures, so I decided to capture it. The reason I am so satisfied with this photograph is because it appears the crab is smiling. Ever since I captured this picture, I make sure I have a camera with me at all times to capture nature's beauty.

ATTERBERRY, BERNADETTE M.

I've been taking pictures for as long as I can remember. I believe the passion began around twelve years old. I carried a camera around with me almost every day, and still do to this day. You just never know when you might capture that one special moment to keep forever. "A Bug's Life" was taken in the summer of 2007 at my husband's Uncle Ronnie's house in Arkansas. We go there every year for a big cookout and family reunion. The landscaping there is really beautiful, so of course I had to take advantage it!

AUTREY, JACKIE

Every year for Valentine's Day my husband and I try to take a trip to Gatlinburg, Tennessee for a romantic getaway. During one of our Valentine trips in 2006, we were driving by the Sugarlands Visitor Center and I happened to notice how wonderful the snow-dusted mountains looked from there. That is when I snapped this photo. Every time I look at this photo, I feel such great peace and thankfulness inside me, because God has given us such beauty for the eye to behold.

BAKER, PATRICK ANTHONY

During a 2006 trip to South America, I was privileged to visit many places. My ship started from Buenos Aires, along the Patagonian Coast to the Falkland Islands. We continued around Cape Horn and along the Chilean Coast to Valparaiso. My photograph was taken on tranquil Lake Esmeralda at Petrohue, Chile. I have visited this lake twice because of its tranquility and captivating energy. I am originally from Jamaica and currently reside in Monterey, California. My interest in photography was born during my teenage years. After traveling throughout Europe, South America, and the United States, my interest became my passion. Landscape and nature photography became my focus. I enjoy sharing my visions through the art of photography and feel honored that my photograph has been considered.

BALDWIN, KELLY MAIRE

This photo is one of my favorite pictures of my rabbit because it shows a side of rabbit behavior that I think many people don't see. His full name is Money The Bunny, and my husband got him for me for my birthday. This is Money's way of showing me some love or just saying, "Hi." I love coming home every day and getting his special greeting. Besides, who doesn't love bunny kisses?

BASHA, FARIDA N.

I relate scents to memory because I always smell fruits, talking about the freshness and the smell of them since I moved to the United States of America six years ago. Every time I see fruits and oranges, I tell my husband about that smell; that's how I have been using my memory to smell. The picture describes when the smell by the memory met the smell of the reality. My husband, Robert B. Basha, and our three-month-old beautiful baby, Sarah Amira Basha, and I went to Algeria, our beautiful country, to visit in January 2007. The first few hours on our way to our hometown, we saw those beautiful, fresh oranges; some people were placing them on the side of the street. We stopped and bought some—they were so fresh and tasty. It was a very beautiful image. That's when I took the picture, and I told my husband, "That's the smell I have been talking about." It was a moment of happiness and I felt the marriage between the smell, the taste, and my memories for six years.

BASS, JOHN CLIFFORD, SR.

Walter D. Bass was born on July 19, 1931. He was not "Father," he was "Daddy," there is a difference. He was Daddy to four sons and four daughters. He was "Grandpap" or "Pappy" to fifteen grandchildren and seventeen great-grandchildren. He was the lover, best friend, and soulmate of his wife of nearly fifty-six years, our mother, Winifred Orlea Cook Bass. God blessed us with loving and caring parents. Mom longs to be with him again. He spent his last years traveling and spending time with his family. On March 11, 2006, he made his final trip home. He was seventy-four years old. "Daddy Smiling" reflects the love and respect we all hold in our hearts for him.

BAXTER, JEANNETTE MARYANNE

I took this photo while holidaying on the island of Vanuatu. My sister and I were there for a friend's wedding and we fell in love with it. I feel like this photo captures the untouched beauty of the island, and it brings back many great memories for me.

BEAUDOIN, ELAINE

This is a photo of Crownsnest Mountain taken from Atlas Flats on a snowy day in October. The snow finally stopped and as the clouds started to break up and the sun tried to shine, I happened to look up at the mountain and saw it peeking through the clouds. I simply thought it would be a nice picture. I live in Crowsnest Pass, Alabama with my husband and two children. I have lived here my entire life and am still constantly amazed by the beauty of the mountains surrounding me.

BECKMAN, TINA

When my husband told me we were going to Alaska I couldn't believe it. After twenty years of talking about it, it was finally a dream come true. I wanted to capture every moment of every second we had there. The glaciers were enormous and sounds were awesome. This picture of a glacier breaking off and going into the ocean and then just floating away seemed surreal, just like life when you grow up and move away. The color in the picture is so true blue, and in person, so breathtaking.

BELCHER, YVETTE

I fell in love with photography when I was around eight years old. Even when I'm not shooting with a camera, I'm still shooting with my mind's eyes. This photo was shot at a zoo. I had to shoot this monkey. It looks as if the monkey is doing the two-step.

BELETSKAYA, MARYANA

This photograph was taken from the rooftop of the Castello Estense in Ferrara, Italy during November 2007. It was a very cold and crisp day and streets in the city were almost empty. I like this photo because it shows the cold enviroment outside the window gate.

BENDALL, SAMUEL WREN

The creation of this image and many others similar to it made me know where I want to take my photography in the future. It was initially an experiment, but ended up taking me down a road where I could find and express my own unique style as an artist. I want to thank my dear friend, Mischa, for being my subject and continually inspiring me as an artist, as well as my parents for continually supporting my creative nature.

BENNER, MARK ALAN

My picture was the result of a May 2006 vacation to visit my mother in beautiful northwest Montana! I have loved eagles and nature my whole life. My mother has lived in Montana for 20 years and I have never visited her by myself until this trip. I know this is an immature bald eagle because they do not aquire their white head and tail feathers until they are four years old. I saw this eagle soaring close to the treetops over and around my mother's house for two days before I took this picture. I took a pair of binoculars and held the lens of the binoculars up to the lens of my Sony FD Mavica digital camera and by accident did not get a good seal of the two lenses, thus giving the picture a "moonlight effect." My mother has never had an eagle land in her yard, but on that day on the trip by myself, it came to pass, and I captured it on film. Be kind to nature, and keep taking pictures.

BENOIT, CHELSEA T.

In my town and surrounding towns, the juniors and seniors can choose to go on a trip to New York or District of Columbia. I chose to go and see the city life of New York. Our guide decided to go to Ellis Island by the ferry. We went by the ferry and passed by the Statue of Liberty. I took several shots as we went by. This was one of the better ones. It includes the Statue of Liberty and surprisingly, an American flag, by coincidence.

BENSON, JEANNIE M.

This is a photo of my oldest son's dog, Max. He was just enjoying a quiet time in the clover after playing hard with our grandchildren. Sometimes you wonder that goes through the mind of an animal. I love taking photos and capturing the perfect moment, like this one of Max.

BERTRAND, FRANCIS PAUL

Sydney, Australia is a city with both old and new architecture that at night melds into a glorious symphony of light and motion. It is appropriate that this photograph was captured on the veranda of the Sydney Opera House. Photography is my passion—I love it.

BIGBY, JENNIFER LYNN

I took this picture at Dow Gardens in Midland, Michigan. My two-year-old daughter, Nia, pointed to the location and wanted me to take a picture. I am glad she did—it turned out wonderful. Nia is now three years old and taking pictures of almost everything in her path. I think she will become an outstanding photographer.

BILLINGHAM, EDWARD ALAN

This picture was taken outside the little town of Torrington, Alberta, Canada. I drive this road all the time. The day this picture was taken, Daisy was looking out the window of my truck at some ducks in the pond. Luckily, I had my camera! I slowed down, hit reverse, unrolled the window, and took a few shots of her sitting in the passenger seat wanting to go say hello.

BILODEAU, MADELEINE CHRISTINE

Every once in a while we find ourselves face to face with a moment when we want a camera to capture the moment. This was one of those times, and thankfully, my camera was right there beside me. It was just an ordinary school morning, waking up at 6:00 a.m., although when I opened the curtains, it seemed surreal. This was a sunrise to never forget.

BLAKELEY, JACKIE YVONNE

I am fourteen and love to take pictures. This is a picture of my dog, Scooter. He loves to have his picture taken. I live in a small town with my loving parents. I hope someday to be a professional photographer. It is a true honor to have my picture published in a book of photography.

BOIVIN, JESSICA ANN

You can take thousands of pictures and only a few will bring out the beauty of the moment. I only get to see my mom's side of the family once every one or two years. So in summer 2007, I became the Paparazzi! I took this picture while I was fiddling around with my camera's settings and my grandpa was, without knowing, my test subject. My mom and my Auntie Mary were playing a game that we like to call "Wacky Golf." Grandpa was sitting on the sidelines, just so intrigued.

BOLING, JASON

I am currently a student at the University of Kentucky studying archeology. This photo was taken on a trip to Bratislava, Slovakia while I was serving in the United States Air Force. My friend and I were walking down one of the many old cobblestone streets when we heard this gentleman playing the violin. After giving him a donation for his humble music, I snapped this photo.

BOS, JAMES J.

I am a retired state trooper who always carries a camera on the job. Digital photography has opened up a new world for me. We live in Michigan, where the winters can often be brutal and beautiful. This was the end of a rough day of snow and wind in January 2007. The sun is breaking through at the end of the day over ice-covered trees and a frozen lake. The serenity, quiet, and beauty could only be caught by a camera.

BOTTONE, ROSEANNE

Emerald green, turquoise, aqua, and cerulean blue flowed and mixed with one another as I departed St. Croix in the United States Virgin Islands. How lucky am I that I was afforded this unique perspective from an eight-seater prop plane flying low over the Caribbean Ocean on a perfect day? To capture this once-in-a-lifetime experience, I grabbed my ordinary point-and-shoot, two-megapixel camera—nothing fancy. No set up—no planning. I was presented with a truly breathtaking moment that filled me with joy and my inspiration was simply to remember.

BOYER, JEFF W.

I took this picture of my grandson when he was one week old. His birthday is June 2, 2006. His name is Liam Boyer and he is number six out of nine grandchildren, for now. I am originally from Calgary, Alberta, Canada and now reside in Dowary, California. Photography is a hobby of mine, and one day I would like to do it fulltime. We welcome all new spirits into our family. I work with Southwest Airlines and love to travel. I love history and love to document it by capturing it on film.

BRANT, LINDA L.

I named this photo after our mother; she passed away December 4, 2007. I took this photo just down the road from her home. I was pleased to spend time with her before she passed away and I had published a book of spiritual poems called "God, I Praise Thee," which I had signed and given to her. She was overjoyed with it. She read the whole book before she left us to go to Heaven.

We miss her and will see her again someday. When I took the picture, I decided right then to name photo after our mother. Thank You, God, for the chance to take this beautiful scene. It was taken in New London, Ohio.

BROMLEY, HOLLY LAURIE

My name is Holly Bromley and I am twenty-four; I will talk about the storm I was in. I live in Calgary, Alberta. I was leaving the gym at five in the evening. It was October 2007 and the strangest thing happened—half of the sky turned jet black, the other half, sunny and blue with no clouds at all. There was a line splitting the sky, and seemed like a battle between darkness and light. Hail poured on one half; I stood in the sun, dry, five feet from the hailstorm, watching rays of fire in the sky. I needed to capture the moment and took this shot with my Palm Treo camera phone. It was beautiful.

BROOKES-TSANG, REBECCA JANE

This photo was taken on my honeymoon in the Maldives. We were on a sunset cruise and the moment was so beautiful. The view of the ocean meeting the sky was overpowering and made us, as people, feel very insignificant. This photo is one of the best examples of my work. My husband and I are graphic designers, but I have been interested in photography since I was about ten and have done it as a hobby ever since. I've recently begun to sell my work and paintings because I want to share them with others.

BROOKMAN, AMY RENEE

My best friend, Ayra Morgan, is the model in the photo and was taken at Henley Beach, Adelaide, Australia. I have had an interest in photography for a few years now. I am twenty-three years old and have always loved to explore new optons with my camera. I especially enjoy photographing the people that mean something to me becasue it gives me great memories.

BROOKS, CURT JAMES

My wife, Sherry, and I have been traveling for over thirty-three years and have been to forty different countries. I have been doing photography for forty years and have accumulated over five thousand pictures. We have lived in Arizona most of our lives and we love to travel, see new places, and meet interesting people. This was our second trip to Alaska and the second time we were able to see this magnificent view of Mount Denali with no cloud cover. When we got within thirty miles, I took this photograph with a 400mm-zoom lens. We were so fortunate to have fantastic weather to view this giant wonder. We are likely to return to this beautiful site again.

BROSCIOUS, JUDY

I have always been interested in photography. I am a divorced mother of two, and a friend of mine taught me about picture composition. I visited Longwood Gardens often. It offers many unique photo opportunities. For my Christmas 2007 trip, I went with my women's social group. When I walked into the conservatory with all the Christmas flowers around, I couldn't resist trying to capture the beauty of this amorilis.

BROWN, A. J.

I am a visual painter artist. I am always taking pictures of my cat to paint. I lucked out with this photo. I had the camera in my hands. I was waiting for something from Rumbles; I had no idea what! I raised my hands to my eyes and clicked the camera as my cat was jumping down. I said to myself, "Oh, I hope that turns out ok!" You can see from the background part of my current work at the time the picture was taken.

BROWN, ANNETTE

Photography is a wonderfully unique form of art that allows others to see how I view the world and people around me. I feel very honored when others appreciate my photographs and the treasures I find in my everyday life. This photo of my son, Adam. He was five years old and trying so hard to be big enough to ride a horse by himself. This photo may lead you to believe that due to his small size, he was perhaps unable to reach the stirrups and ride on his own. In reality, he did do it and I was the one who was not quite ready for him to do it. I am a part-time photographer living in Stonewall, Manitoba, where I operate my own business called Purely Pictures. I have no studio, but specialize in outdoor photography for families, local musicians, bands, and special events.

BROWN, GEOFFREY D.

After buying a new camera, my friend, Ani, and I found a nice spot on a hill to take pictures. The clouds were perfect and the weather warm. We were there for hours enjoying the view until the Astro ruined it for us, and we left.

BRUNST, MARY ELIZABETH

This is a picture of a litter of kittens that are at that uninhibited playful age, where life is simply fun. I am a self-employed, faux-finished artist. I started to greatly enjoy photography after purchasing a DSLR camera to take better quality photographs of my work. Now it has become a hobby that I greatly enjoy and would like to further pursue. I love taking pictures of God's beautiful creations and capturing the candid moments of life.

BUHOCI, CATERINA

This gorilla was in captivity by himself at the time, and what drew me to take his picture was the way he was interacting with people around him. He would sit there and watch us in the same way as we watched him—in languish, awe, and with absolute stillness. Considering our genetic make-up is relatively close to the gorilla and chimpanzee, to wonder if we are the only conscious species on this planet is undeniable when looking at him.

BUJOLD, NOELLA

I love trees. In my mind, live oaks are the most beautiful and majestic of all. They evoke dreams of shaded verandas, mint juleps, and Rhett Butler. I am awed at their ageless endurance. Imagine the joy, excitement, pain, and sorrow they have witnessed in their long years of existence. These particular live oaks are in Brookgreen Gardens in Myrtle Beach, South Carolina. My husband and I never miss a chance of visiting Brookgreen Gardens whenever we are in South Carolina. We enjoy walking through this wonderful sculpture and botanical garden. It is a joy to behold!

BULIANI, STEFANO

Born in 1983 and growing up with a classical education, focused more on education itself rather than schooling, Stefano became a computer programmer in Milan, Italy. Stefano's passion for nature and wildlife photography began early in his life during the long holidays on the Italian Alps with his family. Upon his arrival to London, England, Stefano's interest in photography was

rekindled. He has produced several collections of photographic prints detailing many aspects of his life in London.

BULLER, HALEY

I was in Hawaii with my family enjoying my day when all of a sudden the wind started blowing and blew this flower into the pool. It was so beautiful. It looked like it was alive. The flower floated around the pool for hours. It made people laugh and look at it with big smiles. The next morning ,it was still in the pool. I took it out, laid it in the sun to dry, and then put it in my hair. I wanted something to remember my trip by, and this flower was it.

BUNDA, KAREN LYNN

At the beginning of this year, I lost my brother, Paul. Paul and I shared a love for eagles. On October 3, 2007, I was missing him. I came out of the building where I work at 11:35 a.m. and saw this cloud in the sky. It looked like an eagle to me. It was as if my brother was with me. I took out my camera phone and took a picture. It was like having Paul by my side.

BURDEN, SARA LEE

Ever since I received my first camera at age six, I've had a strong passion for photography. Growing up, being outdoors all the time inspired me to get into nature photography. I love hiking with my fiancé, Drew, and our two dogs, and capturing all the beauty that surrounds us. Elk Falls, Kansas is one of our favorite hikes, and since I carry my camera everywhere, I couldn't help but capture a picture. I run a floral department, and in my spare time I enjoy being with my sisters, Nicole and Tiffany, who encourage and embrace all my photography.

BURDICK, JENNIFER SUSAN

This photo basically sums up my sweet baby, Emma, a smiley, happy girl at heart with an incredible gift to spread her happiness. She is truly a blessing and makes this world a greater place to exist.

BURT, ANN MARIE

This photo was taken at my parents' cottage in Hunstville, Ontario, Canada. I walked by the tree and there he was. I ran and got my camera right away, I just couldn't believe how amazing this picture turned out. It is the backdrop for my computer too. I love photography and I'm thankful for living in such a beautiful country. I'm twenty-eight years old and I live in Bracebridge, Ontario. I've always had a thing for pictures. My living room is full of them. Every time I get a good picture of someone or something, I'm always showing everyone, and now everyone gets to see my "Tree Frog." I hope those who see this picture enjoy it as much as I do.

BUSH, CONNIE S.

My son, Seth, spent hours on the dock that day fishing and then, with no luck, resorted to prayer to catch a fish. He would take a break and come in the cabin to tell me he had been praying for some help. He would say, "I asked God to let me catch a fish just for you, Mom, but He won't let me." This poor child continued trying until it was dark outside. But alas, no fish. The frame of the leaves and the color of the water reflected in the clouds made this truly an amazing photo and a precious memory.

BUSTOS, LILIANA

Inspired by beautiful scenery and breathtaking trees, this shot was quickly snapped of a serene woodpecker at a rest stop in Sequoia National Park. The attraction was obvious, the iredescent blue feathers of this uninhibited creature were emphasized by the contrast against the weathered, chocolate step. It was more than an ordinary bird, it was an extraordinary depiction of nature at its best. I look forward to continuing my quest to find beauty in nature.

BUTLER, MIKE

I enjoy taking pictures to use as computer desktop backgrounds. "Red Tree With Vine" was taken on one of our family walks through a local state park.

BUXAR, TERESIA JANA

It was a hot summer evening, and we decided to go to the lake, where the sun was slowly setting. My brother was fishing, my parents were sitting on a big rock enjoying the sunset, and my sister was throwing pebbles at the lake to make rebounds. The camera was in my hands, so I took a chance to take a nice picture. What a memory!

CACIOPPO, ELEANOR CAROLINE

Due to circumstances beyond my control, I had to move 1,200 miles from my grandchildren. I miss them all so much, especially my youngest grandaughter, Joelle, who was always with me. They had this expression about me, "Our Grammy doesn't even go to the bathroom without her camera!" God is so good—one of the things He gave me in this hard move was a house surrounded by woods. My photo, "Mommy And Me," was taken from my window. I have countless more, just ask my grandkids.

CALVELAGE, CHARISSA ANN

This photo was taken in northern Maine while I was doing a traveling contract. I'm a traveling nurse and I get to go to all sorts of wonderful and unique places. I take pride in trying to find the real beauty in nature. I was driving around and enjoying the view when I drove past this gorgeous tree. I had to make three passes to get just the right shot. I hope you love it as much as I do.

CANTRELL, COURTNEY SHEA

I have always loved to watch the sunrise over the ocean. This trip to Cumberland Island was my daughter's first time being able to play in the water because she had just learned to walk two months before our trip. Alle loved the water, and it was so beautiful to see her little footprints in the sand and reflection in the water as she walked around. I had to capture this moment because she is growing so fast. This photo shows me just how big God is in His beautiful creation.

CAPPARELLI, JOHN M.

When it comes to hiding, Mimi loves to play peek-a-boo. She's constantly jumping out from the covers to surprise me with her presence. This photo was taken to show just how much fun she is

to have in my life, and around the house every day! Truly, I'm blessed to have her! Mimi is a great older sister as well as a great younger sister, but she is truly a "Daddy's girl." Since the picture was taken, she has grown into a healthy one-year-old. She is a winner to me always and forever, and my best friend to the end. I guess I really love her and I hope you guys looking at this picture see what I see—a beautiful, spunky, elegant cat that's going to keep me busy for years to come. She's my baby girl, and my princess!

CARO, SUSAN

I took this shot while I was volunteering on a lion reserve in South Africa. I had just given the lion I was playing with a kiss on the nose, and I guess he liked the lip gloss I was wearing, because he licked his nose right after. For as long as I can remember, my camera has always felt like it was a part of me, almost like it was my right arm. I love to took at the world through my camera lens and see what interesting and beautiful images I can capture.

CASH, SCOTTYE J.

This was my first photography trip to capture something besides flowers or my dogs. This photograph is of a mother chimpanzee at the zoo. There was something about this chimpanzee that captured my attention and evoked many different thoughts. I see the unique soul of an animal and how animals have such an amazing impact on our lives. I also see the eyes of a mother and all that being a mother involves and the possible sadness of being a captive animal. The title, "In The Eye Of The Beholder," reflects an understanding that this photo may touch each person differently.

CASTRO, MICHELLE MARIE

This is a picture of my three-year-old son, Jordan Ray, by Silverwood Lake, California. This was his first time on a boat and he was so excited to be out in the lake. I took this picture to capture the fascination he had "by the lake."

CERAVINO, CLAIRE

Photography has been my passion for many years. My family and friends are used to me having a camera in my hands and my children always tried to stay out of the line of fire. I have been lucky to have several of my pictures chosen over the years, but "Bermuda Dreams" holds a special place in my heart. On July 7, 2007, my youngest daughter, Tracey, was married to Rick in Bermuda, with this in the background. What a perfect setting. Having this photo chosen makes the event even more special.

CHAFFEE, CORY

I've been taking photographs for as long as I can remember., but until my son, Ryly, came into the picture, my talent seemed to be lacking. Ryly is the joy in my life and is always ready to amaze me and everyone in the photographs I have taken of him these past years. I love you, "bug."

CHANEY, GREG A.

This is my former scoutmaster and friend, Denis Porterin, in his blown and alcohol-injected jet boat, "Butterfly." "Butterfly's" top speed is 144 mph and is the 2007 National Jet Boat Association

8.0-8.499 second-bracket winner. Stephen Stuart, in the orange boat, is the 2007 National Jet Boat Association 9.5-9.999 second-bracket winner with a top speed of 118 mph. This picture captures one of the qualifying runs that took place at the N.J.B.A. drag meet, at Ming Lake in beautiful Bakersfield, California.

CHAPMAN, ADAM GRANT

I took this photo while on a walk around the camp I worked at over the summer. The camp is located in the town of Toalmas, Hungary. The photo is of a blue sailor, a common wildflower that can even be found in my home state of Tennessee. It's funny how you can see something all the time and not really notice it. Then, you see it in a different place or different situation that helps you to see how beautiful it really is. It helps you to appreciate it. Take the time to notice what's around you or what you have and appreciate it.

CHENG, ANDREW KA HO

During the 2007 summer, I went back to Hong Kong and this picture was taken in a place called Stanley. This is a very well known tourist spot in Hong Kong and it has some gorgeous buildings and a fantastic beach which you can spend your whole day relaxing and enjoying your vacation. There is a row of bars and restaurants along Stanley's waterfront, and I have spent some wonderful moments with my friends which give me precious memories.

CHIRICO, DINA ANN

This was taken at Fort Mifflin in Philadelphia, Pennsylvania while beginning a paranormal investigation. The fort is adjacent to the Philadelphia International Airport, so planes are constantly landing and taking off. I thought taking this picture with the ground archway would be interesting and unique. When taking pictures of nature and/or incorporating moving images, I try to capture the extraordinary or just the ordinary in a different light. I'm a taste-tester for Mars Incorporated and an energy healer living in Warren County, New Jersey with my husband, son, and stepson.

CHOUDHURY, FARHANA S.

During my visit to my mother's house back in Bangladesh, I was recalling the memories of my childhood on her terrace. While gazing out to the sunset, I noticed two birds resting on an electrical wire. They too, like myself, were watching the sunset. It was an amazing moment. I instantly took a picture. I have a passion for capturing the world's beauty of nature.

CHU, RICHARD L.

This picture was taken in a New York state park concessions building. The dark, abandoned room stores forgotten machinery, dust, junk, and other unused objects. While the sight of this spectacular room and everything in it intrigued me, this rusted safe captivated my eyes the most—the opened safe seems to give a post-apocalyptic impression. Highlighted by the light of day, the abandoned safe is the most conspicuous object in the room with an aura of solitude and mystery surrounding it.

CLARKE, KAYE ALISON

I am an Australian living an adventure in Canada. I came to Canada in January 2004 to work as a registered nurse in Yellowknife, Northwest Territories. This photo was taken at sunrise of a tower from the hospital where I worked. It is, of course, winter, and the temperature was negative 40 degrees celsius. I love photography, and capturing landscapes on film is my specialty.

CLIFFORD, BEN GEORGE

This is a photo of my cousin, Siena, at age three. She's in a completely different world, sitting with her breakfast and daydreaming. She thinks she looks sad. I was suprised at how good this image looked in black and white; it has an entirely different feel when printed in color. I have enjoyed taking photos from an early age, which really became a big interest of mine when I studied photography for two years at 'A'-level. Now, I always have a camera with me, waiting for that perfect photo opportunity like this one.

CLISBY, LORESSA ANITA

I have traveled since I was a child and visited many places around the globe. I studied photography at a university and always take my camera wherever I go. I journeyed to Venice during winter. It was shrouded in fog and quite cold, but I was captivated by the contrasts of the wonderful architectural craftmanship and their inevitable decay as the rising tides over the years have forced people to brick up their doorways. You could see where the water line had reached several feet up the gilded mosaic walls in Basilica. This photo represents my glimpse into that world.

CLOUTIER, MICHAEL

Being a young, nineteen-year-old artist finishing my studies in graphic arts, I have to surpass myself in different areas. Up until now, I managed to master media such as drawing, painting, airbrush, and everything connected to publicity and graphic design. But of all these medias, photography hit me the hardest. I'm honored that others liked my work. The picture was taken in a moment of solitude. I often go to calm places to find inspiration. One day, I got to this place and observed the night on one side and sunset on the other. I had to immortalize this moment of beauty. I'm happy to share those feelings with you. All existences, all things have a beauty and positive side, we only have to bring it out.

COGBURN, DONITA

I was going home from work when I stopped beside the road to take a nice picture of a cloud with the sun just shining underneath. When I snapped the shot, the cloud moved and I got the full sun. I snapped the picture with my cell phone just outside of Sidney, Texas. When I had the picture developed, everyone was amazed at the way there was a purple ring underneath. I thought it looked like what Heaven would look like if it was open and welcoming people home.

COLLINS, CHRISTOPHER O'NEAL

Photography is my passion. I have loved photography since the very first time I picked up a camera. Growing up in rural southwest Mississippi, there was always something catching my eye that I would want to capture on film. This is a photograph taken of my ninety-four-year-old grandfather's hands during an afternoon visit. I entitled this photo "Hands Of Unity," because my grandfather is the one who keeps the family bond strong. His hands reflect years of hard work and future family generations represented by the wedding band on his right hand.

COOPER, JUNE RADER

My mother was born on this farm on June 15, 1921. In September 2007, the doctors told us she had about three months to live after she was operated on for colon cancer. My two brothers and I chose to care for her at home so she could remain on the farm she loved. I would go out every morning and take a photo of the sunrise. On February 22, 2008 the sun set for our mother and God took her home. We were very lucky children to have this wonderful person for our mother.

CORSETTO, AMY BETH

The army stationed our family in the Bavarian area of Germany in 2004. To remember this wonderful experience, I kept a record of my daily life and the wonderful sites through pictures. This picture is taken from my backyard during one of our winters in Germany.

COSTA, TRISH

I'm a stay-at-home mom who enjoys photography. I have two sons, Justin, twelve, and Nathan, nine. When they are both in high school and with the support of my husband, Nelson, I plan on taking photograpy classes. This picture was taken at the Toronto Zoo. When I saw the flower bed, I noticed right away the beauty of this flower. When I got home, I blew it up to an 8x10, now it hangs in the kitchen wall. I've had a lot of compliments on it, so I decided to share its beauty with you all.

COURSOLLE, CARRIE ANN

This is a photo of my little cousin, Morgan. She's quite photogenic—it's really hard to take a bad picture of her. This one just happened to outshine them all.

COX, ERIN ELIZABETH

I took this picture at a park near the hotel where I used to work in downtown Montreal. It was just after the firt snowfall in December 2006, and I just loved the look of it. The benches were all lined up and nobody was around. I have been taking photos since I was fourteen and I absolutely love it. I love capturing something somebody else might not see. I bring my camera almost everywhere because you never know what will happen.

CRABTREE, TRACY L.

I was on a trail ride with my mom. We passed by this pretty scene and took a random photo. When I got home and loaded it on my computer, it was so pretty, I wanted to share it. The only way it would be better is if their was a horse in it.

CRANE, SUZANNE GAIL

When my husband and I moved to Searchmont I fell in love with the beauty of our new home and its surroundings. We live on 18.6 acres of land surrounded by eleven mountains on the fork of two rivers. What more could an artist ask for? This is what I call "Wenaki," meaning, "place of sanctuary." It is my husband's and my home away from home. We love Wenaki.

CRAWFORD, BLANDYE J.

This picture was taken one afternoon while my family and I were swimming. Rye was two years old in this shot and loving the water. His face says it all.

CREWS, RANDALL JAY

This is one of the first photos I took as a photographer, so it means a lot to me. Every time I look at it, I am reminded of when I started photography and the passion I have developed for it since.

CREWS, RANDALL JAY

This photo is of my boyfriend, Andrew, taken to promote his musical career. I love the complexity of the photo because of all the lines. This photo developed new relationships in my life and I consider it one of my favorite works.

CROOKS, MATTHEW BRIAN

My picture, "Summer Bloom," is a testament to my parents for the beauty in life that they have taught me to see.

CRUTCHFIELD, JONNA

My beautiful son, Thomas Edward Johnson II, was five months old at the time this picture was taken. He was just so precious on this day, I had to take a picture of his sweet little face as he smiled at me with all the love in the world a son could give his mother.

CUDAHY, LAURIE

My love for photography came from my father. I got bit by the "photography bug!" This photo was taken when my husband and I were on a road trip with our Corvette Club. We were traveling from Southern California to Breckenridge, Colorado. I snapped this picture on the day we were traveling from Saint George, Utah to Parachute, Colorado.

CUNNINGHAM, MOLLY JOY

Here in wild and wonderful West Virginia, we grow some beautiful blossoms. This adorable bloomer is my daughter, ViviAnne, at eight months old. April showers bring May flowers, and August heat brings a cooling treat when my daughter took her first dip in her pool. This picture is my "flower child" drying off with miles of smiles. ViviAnne is my first and only child, so I make it a point to always have a camera on hand to capture all of the memories that I can!

CUNNINGHAM, SAMANTHA

I have always liked taking photos of nature, especially flowers. When I found some tiger lilies on my school campus, I felt like I needed to take a picture. The colors were just so vibrant and there were such details on the petals that it seemed wrong not to capture them. Even though the flowers are off to the right, the neutral green background makes them standout. You can never know what's out in the environment until you really look. You might find the beautiful things in a sea of the ordinary.

DANIELS, TERESA ANN

Not being one to sit around much, I thought my life was confined to watching the grass grow when rheumatoid arthritis came to stay ten years ago. My husband, Rod, encouraged my picture taking, which not only got me up and going, but opened a world of pleasure and satisfaction. It's amazing how sometimes subtle changes in nature can make the picture you take "pop!" This small creek on our place has always been a reliable subject for me and this day was no exception.

DAPPEN, ALEX

I took this picture at the world-renowned Crankworx Biking Festival this year in Whistler, British Columbia. The picture is of famous rider, Kyle Strait, transferring from a quarter pipe. The festival was a great opportunity for me to work on action shots because the spectators were allowed to walk the length of the course and stand next to all the jumps. It was a great experience to be so close to all the action. I am a student studying photography and journalism at Northern Arizona University in Flagstaff, Arizona.

DARNELL, PEARCE DAVID

As a child, I was always inspired by art—drawing, sketching, and painting. As I reached adulthood, I finally found the right art medium—photography! Photographing is very spiritual for me. God leads and guides me. He reveals His beautiful creation to me, and the images are born. God is truly an artist, as He uses me for His purpose!

DAVIDSON, KENNA R.

This is a photo of our special three-year-old miniature Schnauzer, Megan, that displays her unique appreciation for hibiscus blooms. This photo was completely spontaneous as we captured her concentrated effort to reach the red bloom that remained out of paw's reach. This photo is a special treasure to my husband, Gary, and me that we'll enjoy for years to come.

DEDONA, ROSEANNE

This photograph was taken after a great weekend visiting Niagara Falls, Ontario. As we drove across the Rainbow Bridge and headed east toward New York, I took one last look at the sky over Canada and snapped this picture.

DEJACOMO, CLARE TERRY

The picture is my husband when we went on our one and only cruise for three days. They took us up to the top to show us how to put the life jackets on and where to go to the lifeboats. I told him to stand there so I could take his picture, and when I was ready, this is what he did. I thought it was very funny and everybody was hysterical. And that was my husband, always fooling around. Unfortunately, July 3, 2006 he passed away, so I was so thrilled when I got your letter. All I can say is he's still here with me. Thank you so much. You know I'm an artist, not a photographer so this is really great—a real honor.

DELANEY, BILL

My friend, Pat Bodner, photographed my cat, Shania, and gave it to me and I named it "The Country Cat." I want my friend to get credit for photographing my cat. These are my pictures.

DELAUDER, SHERRY ANNE

As an elementary teacher, I am constantly snapping pictures of my students in action, just as I caught my children growing up; however, my grown children are far better photographers than I. "Caught You!" was the result of my determination to get a picture of my only granddaughter smiling before she flew 3,000 miles to her home. Abby is curious about everything, especially if it is off-limits. When I noticed that she was in my plant room, I snuck up on her sending her, into gales of giggles and smiles this picture.

DELESBORE, SHARON JUANITA

It is always beautiful to see a father teaching his son how to be a man. This is what I captured when I snapped this shot on a whim. Seeing my two men interact together is always overwhelming to me because it exemplifies love. Paul Sr. is a wonderful dad who believes that a real man raises his son. I will always cherish this precious moment in time as our family continues to live, love, and learn together.

DELTCHEVA, ILIANA G.

This is a photo of downtown Chicago. I was there with my daughter, Viki, and my best friend, Ivan Lalev. It shows the beauty and the soul of the town so we can keep it forever in our hearts.

DEMBOSKI, JAMES MICHAEL

My dad was a "rockhound," God rest him. "Winter Solace" is my tribute to his memory. My love for him is as solid as a rock, and enduring the cold emptiness of his passing will last until the end of time. Without him, I would not be me.

DEON, EUGENIE MARIE

"Our Little Santa," is a picture of our seven-month-old son, Garrett. It was one of many taken of him in his Santa suit. It was captured with a big smile as Daddy said hello to him. This is a first Christmas and a photo that will always make Daddy and Mommy smile, and a great start to baby Garrett's memories. I love taking photos of my son, family, and outings to use for scrapbooking. I'm very proud and honored that my son's photo has been chosen to be published.

DESJEAN, JESSICA PAIGE

I absolutely love taking photographs, especially of children. "Baby Blues" is a photo of my little brother, Brandon, when he was three years old. We had been living apart at the time and this was our summer together, which I used to take as many pictures of him as I possibly could. He was getting particularly exasperated at my camera when he made that face, so I quickly snapped a shot. It is definitely my favorite photo of him! I'm lucky now to be living near him again in Massachusetts with my boyfriend, Wayne, and my cat, Finley.

DEWINDT, KRISSY

This is a picture of our beautiful daughter, Hannah, playing in the bathtub. Hannah is our first child and was only ten months old at the time the picture was taken. All her pictures are very special, but we picked this one because her eyes look so beautiful.

DILLARD, AMANDA KATE

This picture was taken the day my two-day-old son, Dallas', lung collapsed. He had to get a tube put in to help him breathe. Dallas was seven weeks early and having trouble breathing on his own. So the name of the picture was only obvious—"Holding On For Life." He is now ten months old and you would never know that he was premature. I also have a twenty-two-month-old daughter, KaityLyn, who was also born six weeks premature.

DISHER, TARA-LYNN

This unique photograph was taken in Venice, Italy near San Marco Square. It was an amazing experience to travel such a beautiful country!

DUMFORD, AARON J.

This photo was captured during my first outing with my D40X.

EASTERLY, SARAH

This is a picture I took one morning as I was taking my children, Kelsie and Dalton, to school. I love to take pictures, so my husband, Darrell, suggested that I put "Sunrise" on Picture.com so others could enjoy the beauty of nature. Most of all, I think God deserves all the praise and glory because He is the real photographer of this beautiful sunrise. I just had the camera!

EDGINGTON, BARBARA HALE

My father gave me my first camera. He told me that if I paid attention, I'd always come across an interesting shot. Ever since digital technology, I've saved so much because I take pictures constantly! I have four adopted animals that have given me some pretty amazing pictures. This is of my oldest two Max and Petey, enjoying the evening air, and contemplating life. I feel honored that you found substance in my photograph.

ELDRED, TARA LOUISE

When I took this photo, I was at our local cemetary visiting my friend's, who had very recently passed away, resting site. I had decided to bring my camera that day and came upon the Mother Mary statue. I thought it was so beautiful and meaningful, especially considering everything that I had just gone through.

EMERSON, CHALLAINE MORGAN

This image was captured in Puerto Vallarta, Mexico from my facing balcony. To my amazement, there was a break in the powerful storms, and in an instant, the beauty of the skies and hillsides had revealed themselves. I knew it was a once-in-a-lifetime opportunity, so I had to make sure this majestic moment in time was one I could see again and again. I am a twenty-two-year-old photograher of CME Photography Inc. based in Calgary, Alberta, Canada. I hope to instill in my children the diversity of this wonderful art form so that it can be practiced in my family for many generations to come.

ENRIQUEZ, CARL

This photograph was taken at sunset in the Philippines at the conclusion of a family reunion a beautifully fitting end to a merry occasion.

ESNEAULT, SUZETTE MARIE

I love taking pictures of my children. This picture was taken in Orange Beach, Alabama coming off the beach. This is just one of the many photographs that we captured there. After all, a picture is worth a thousand words, but are also priceless memories to me.

ESPOSITO, LISA ANNE

This photo is our of my five-month-old daughter, Gianna, that was snapped in the backseat of our car. She is always having her picture taken, especially by her brothers, and is not camera shy. My husband, Joe, and I have four children altogether; thirteen-year-old Nicholas, eleven-year-old Joseph Jr., ten-year-old Christopher, and Gianna is the youngest and the only girl, or should I say princess. Although Gianna has some medical problems, she never ceases to amaze us with her spirit. We all adore her and even people that don't know her seem to gravitate toward her. I mean, just look at that smile. Who could resist?

ESTEBAN, SUWELA

April, my Golden Retriever, is seven years, and Leilani, the Labrador, is eight years. Both of the dogs were born in February. Our family celebrates their birthdays every year. They love taking pictures and eating cake.

EYRICH, PETER J.

When people mention the word reflection, what is it that comes to mind? Is it a way in which you think about the past? Is it a way in which we see ourselves, a reflection? Or is it the way an image can be distorted through different mediums? When I hear the word reflection, I think of this photo and the good times associated with living so close to a major city like Philadelphia. The times I think of most are those I spent with my two best friends exploring the city and the feeling we had of infiniteness.

EZERINS, DILLON JOHN

I took this picture when I was on the Gold Coast of Australia. Three of my friends and I took a ride over to Fraser Island by ferry in an eleven-person truck packed with camping gear. This was the morning after the first of our three-night stay, where I spent it sleeping on the roof of our vehicle. The only reason I was awake to see the sunrise is due to the pack of wild dingoes that were invading our camp, stealing some food, but more importantly, our keys.

FAFARD, KINA L.

My nephew, who is only twelve years old, was diagnosed with juvenile diabetes when he was five years old, so we walked for two years with the Diabetes Walk people and I took pictures of the kids. I picked this photo of my daughter, Martika, because I thought it was beautiful and different and so innocent-looking. I love to take pictures. I am a hair dresser, but my hobby is taking pictures. I have five children and I try to catch a lot of memories.

FAIN, STACIE LYNN

This photo was taken in beautiful Juneau, Alaska. I lived there for four years and still visit often. I believe it is one of the most breathtaking places on Earth. This photo was taken in August from the Dyke Trail. You can tell summer is almost over because the fireweed blooms are almost to the top of the stalks. You can also see the Juneau International Airport and the Mendenhall Glacier in the background.

FAIRBRUN, GRANT E.

This is one of the first pictures I took with my new digital camera. I had shot film for years and I am glad I made the switch. This photo couldn't have turned out better. Just outside of Jasper, Alberta there is a place called Maligne Canyon. I stopped there a few times to break up a road trip. It's a place I feel at peace. I had to climb over the pathway barrier to get the right angle. Every time I view this photo, I feel at peace. Now I will always have a place of "serenity!"

FALGOUT, RACHEL CONCETTA

"Daibutsu" is a Japanese term meaning, "Great Buddha." The statue was built in 1252 A.D. and stands 37-feet tall. I visited Kamakura, Japan in the fall of 2006 and felt so at peace watching everyone pray to the Great Buddha. It is a trip I will never forget.

FALSETTI, KAYLA DAWN

Taking pictures is more than a hobby. It's a way to express myself. It allows me to capture the moment and keep it frozen in time, such as this photo from Huntington Beach, where the light shining through the clouds filled me with awe. A sunset, so often taken for granted in such a busy world, is one of the small things in life that I've learned is worth slowing down to enjoy.

FELDSTEIN, MICHAEL

Picturesque sunsets are not something most associate with New York City, yet one evening late in August, Mother Nature painted a masterpiece for the city dwellers with the wherewithal to look up. I was simply driving west in my convertible with the top down when the traffic light guided my attention vertically. In a New York minute, I grabbed my camera, snapped the shot and was on my way.

FERENC, JILL MELANIE

Some say Paris is the city of romance; I say it's the city of fabulous photography opportunities! While strolling through the Musee d'Orsay one afternoon during one of my many museum visits, I couldn't believe my eyes when I saw what some would call a "photographer's dream" standing before me. While I only consider myself an amateur in the photography world, I have been presented with many fortunate circumstances that have led me to take some unbelievable photos. For the meanwhile, I will continue searching for that next great shot on my travels.

FIANDER, JOAN

I have been taking photographs as a hobby since the 1970s. The majesty of Mother Nature fascinates me. I love the challenge of capturing her in all of her beauty and abundance. I like to take the time to get a photograph right. Life changes instantly and I try to capture these moments as they pass in the blink of an eye. I enjoy the challenge of producing a published photograph without the aid of Photoshop. All of my photographs are totally untouched other than cropping, and I'm proud of that.

FINCH, AUGUSTINA

I enjoy taking pictures of sunsets and lots of other sky shots—they intrigue me. But you can only imagine how excited I was when this one came back as good as it did. I take a lot of shots just driving down the road.

FINCH, CHANNING BRIANNE

I'm proud to say this is my first photo to be published. It was taken winter 2007 at Englewood High School. I tend to find my inspiration from loved ones around me. During the time this picture was taken, I was with my boyfriend, Patrick. I'd like to dedicate this photo to all my loved ones—my mother, my boyfriend, and a dear friend, Haley, who recently passed. I find so much joy in photography. I hope to continue publishing my photos.

FLURY, KATHI

I have been an amateur photographer for many years. I adopted little Mitzi over three years ago, and I must say, she has completely changed my life. I have taken many photo of Mitzi, but this photo captured my heart! Words cannot describe the joy "my little Mitzi" has brought to my life and the lives of many others.

FONTANA, GIOVANNI

I come from an artistic background, and I am a musician and a painter. I was born in Milan and moved to Tuscany in the 1980s. I grew up in a community where about 350 people live together. I got my first camera, a Pentax, when I was fifteen and since then, my interest began in photography. I always wanted to travel and left Italy five years ago. This photo is one of many taken on my trips around the globe. Captured on an expedition to one of the highest peaks of the Himalaya in Nepal, I saw the young lad running around in the village, and as he stopped, I photographed him.

FORREST, KEITH W.

The girl in the picture is Monique, she is from Amsterdam. I met her through a mutual friend online and after ten months of chatting, we finally got to meet in person. Monique came to Canada twice to visit me, and finally I went back to Holland with her to see her world. Monique is an awesome young lady, always up for a good laugh. We still keep in touch and hope to holiday together again one day. I will always treasure the time we have spent together.

FRANCK, ELIZABETH JO

I love taking pictures of my cat, Felix. Most of the pictures I take of him are usually the type of pictures that make you want to jump into it and just cuddle with the cute cat. This picture was probably the most amusing of him. I woke up one morning, rolled over, and caught my Felix with my McDonalds' cup, and just had to capture the moment.

FRANCOEUR, CHARLOTTE A.

I am so excited that you have chosen one of my photos for publication. Thank you for giving amateur photographers a place to show their work. I love photographing wildlife, and I was outside photographing the birds at my feeders and my pug, Peanut, was playing in the snow nearby. I had stopped photographing the birds to look for her and there she was with her snowy face sitting about three feet from me watching my horses. I couldn't resist snapping this photo of her. I can't wait for my copy of the book to arrive to see Peanut's photo in print, as well as the work of other amateur photographers.

FRANK, BRIAN S.

I received a digital camera from my parents about one year ago. Since that time, I have been inseparable from my camera. I am always on the hunt for visually pleasing and unique shots. I hope you enjoy this close-up of a praying mantis. It was shot on a picnic table outside my work in Marietta, Georgia. I was very surprised that she let me get as close as she did. It's alien-looking, don't you think?

FRANKHAM, CASSANDRA LEIGH

This photograph took place on a hot summer evening on my way back to British Columbia. I just caught the last glimpse of a forest fire, with the smoke still lingering in the air. The sun was shining like a star as it set on the Western horizon. I saw this as a picture-perfect moment to capture the beautiful tragedy of the remains of a forest fire and a golden sun hanging in the sky.

FREEMAN, KAITLIN DANONE

In life it seems there are those few rare moments when a scene so spectacular unfolds before our eyes. "Once Upon A Time" is one of such moments taken at sunset in Cozumel, Mexico. There is no other story behind it except that of your own imagination. Thanks goes to God for making such a perfect scene. Thank you, Heather, for modeling for me. Lastly, thanks to my parents for always encouraging me with my photography.

FULLEN, SANDY DEE

This picture was taken at Lake Buchanan, off the boat ramps of Black Rock Park. I have always had a great love for photography. My husband and three boys are the love of my life, and for every moment I capture on film, it lives forever in our lives.

GADD, JERRY L.

While gathering ideas for sketching and painting, I came upon a pair of Canadian geese. I was lucky enough to capture the detail and beauty of the birds taking flight. I'm an artist and spend a lot of time outdoors. Sometimes I am able to get an exceptional photograph, and this one certainly fits that description.

GALLAWAY, JAIME SUE

My family has been racing for over fifty years and is still going strong. So it's no surprise that my two-year-old daughter, Adaysia, enjoys watching and cheering for her family. Hopefully she will become the family's next driver and continue the tradition. Photography is another family tradition, and I enjoy taking pictures of my daughter. This is one of my favorites, and I am honored to be able to share it with everyone. Go Team Mopar!

GANDALONE, ALYSE NICHOLE

Dancing to their own song, singing to their own notes, it was otherworldly. Standing there, witnessing these two beautiful creatures grow closer to each other was completely the most peaceful and serene experience I could have asked for. The word "beautiful" means a great deal, but what I captured here appears to be so much more than that. Such a connection sparked between these graceful animals will never compare to anything we know. As humans, we expect to discover a companion to be by our side and share this kind of bliss with—it's just a matter of meeting them.

GANJE, CANDACE LEE

This photo was taken on New Year's Day, a day full of sunshine and newly fallen snow from a snowstorm the night before. My friends and I decided to take a walk in the snow and enjoy the beautiful day and the start of a new year. The photo was taken in Hayward, Wisconsin, on Chief Lake, where we have a small cabin. I take my camera everywhere and love photography. I share my photos with friends and family, as they know my camera is always with me.

GARDNER, TONYA A.

This is one of my twelve grandchildren, and all you have to do is look at her smile and your troubles will disappear. It was just one of those moments when you had to grab your camera. We have beautiful memories of all our grandchildren.

GARIBAY, LOURDES

My name is Lourdes Garibay, and I am from Visalia, California. I'm twenty-six and married with three children. This is a photo of my children walking for the first time on the beach. They enjoyed that day so much and still talk about it to this day.

GATLING, STACY JEANNE

I spent a weekend with my mom taking pictures of a hummingbird and her babies in a tree in my mother's front yard. The bird has been nesting in this tree for two years now. We went out several times to look and take pictures. I was on my grandfather's old, rickety wooden ladder with my digital camera, climbing ever higher as my mother frantically kept telling me to be careful. This was very exciting for me. I am so grateful for being able to zoom into scenes that I have never seen before. Photography allows me to see and experience things that otherwise I could not. I was dancing because I could actually see. I am visually handicapped due to ocular albinism.

GERAUD, MAURICE FRED

My dog, Jacques Cousteau Geraud, is a Maltese-poodle mix born January 1, 1999, and was named after Jacques Cousteau because he is an explorer like Cousteau. You can see it in his eyes. In 2004, when my dog, Jacques, was five years old, I purchased a new Toyota Solara and the DMV sent me a license plate that read, "5JOC555." He is a good dog and it is a good car.

GERIN, PATRICIA ANN

This is a photo of my cat, Opie. Opie loves shoes, and is always "trying them on." Opie is a rescued animal who was dumped at our local cat rescue agency. He loves a warm lap and is very affectionate. He has three cat siblings, two of which are also rescued animals, and a dog friend who was also rescued. All of these animals allow my family to live with them. My human family is my husband, Dan, and our two sons, Sean and Ryan.

GERRISH, JESSICA L.

This is a photo captured from a place that means the world to me. My grandmother owns this land on a lake in Maine. She has a camp that my family and I visit all year long. I have been going there since I was a baby. My uncle even has a camp up the road. I love going to camp and laying in the hammock or going swimming. I always feel inspired when I go there; I wouldn't trade this place for anything.

GETHERS, KHADIJAH

This picture is important because it's a picture of me proving to myself that anything I set my mind to, I can do with a little bit of faith. I set a goal and now I'm living it as a model. This picture also shows the happiness I'm experiencing. No goal is too high!

GHARIOS, KARIM PIERRE

I am Lebanese and lived in Dubai for five years. I was lucky to be able to travel around the world from there. In all the cities I've visited, I always looked to catch the "soul" of the place I'm in, through the lens of a camera. I took this picture of Dubai two months before I moved to Canada. For some reason, the "soul" of Dubai and many other cities remains in my heart. I would like to dedicate this picture to my father, Pierre Georges Gharios, whose unconditional love got me to where I am today. "What you see is not always what is, and what is, you cannot always see."

GIANFALLA, MELISSA ANN

This photo was taken on a trip with my photography class to Saint Joseph's College for a photo shoot. I took this picture because I loved how the water looked. The water had reflections of the trees from above and had ripples far out into the lake. I also loved how the dock looked as you gazed out at it and the lighting was perfect for this type of picture.

GLAUSER, MANDI

This photograph is one of many photographs taken in the Rocky Mountains of central Idaho where I was lucky enough to grow up. I am currently studying photography at the University of Colorado HSC in Denver. Photography is my passion. I love all types of subjects and will for the rest of my life.

GORSKI, SHANE

Lake Lugano proved to be an interesting place. It had many gorgeous buildings, incredible people, and the most upscale McDonald's you'll ever see! I was walking along the shore when I imagined how this final image would look like through my camera and I captured the moment. The look of the foreboding clouds is such a contrast to the colorful coastline of Lugano. As an inspiring freelance photographer, I hope to ignite the fire in the bellies of people that procrastinate to travel. Go now, experience it, and tell everyone about it!

GREGERSEN, TABATHA ANN
I took this picture while working with my daughter, Natasha, and niece, Sabrina. We had seen this part of the "ghost train" and decided to take a picture with the girls on it. This part of the train no longer runs and is what we call the "ghost train."

GREIN, SHAUN PERRY
My name is Shaun Grein. I live in Lethbridge, Alberta, Canada. This photo was taken in the summer, while I was in the middle of training. My family is camera-happy, and I was asked to pose for them.

GRESENS, WILLIAM A.
I've been in the navy for fourteen years, and on my third deployment to the Persian Gulf, my ship stopped here in Darwin, Australia for a port visit. I had just bought a brand-new camera at my last port visit in Hawaii, which has a sunset mode, and as you can see, it paid off really well.

GUL, PELIN
This photo was taken in 2005 when I was wandering around by myself on my university's campus in a late afternoon. All of a sudden, I noticed this little hole on a wall when I was passing by. The hole was a little high, so I had to climb some stairs to see what was behind it. The scene through it was incredibly serene and peaceful and I started daydreaming while enjoying this view. I kept staring from this little hole for a while. I had my camera with me and I wanted to shoot this hole and its scene so that I could look at my photo anytime to have a little bit of peace.

GUTH, JAMES ALAN
This is a photo that was taken during a road trip along the Blue Ridge parkway. The location of the photo is near the Wash Creek Overlook in North Carolina.

GUZMAN, TIERRA NOELLE
I'm fourteen. This picture of the ocean was taken on a Sunday in Santa Cruz, when I went to relax with my dad. I take pictures of nature and animals mostly, so when I went to Santa Cruz and saw this beautiful day, I had to take a picture. In doing so, I captured a bird and a sunray in the picture.

HALEY, ALAN J.
I took this photograph, and I love how people continue to admire it. It was my grandma's birthday, and we stopped at the lake for some ice cream as the sun set. At the edge of the water, I noticed my two little cousins looking off into the sunset. I snuck up behind them to capture the picture, without disrupting them. What they were talking about as they pointed off to the sunset, I'll never know, but what I do know is that it's the best photograph I've ever taken.

HALLIBURTON, JASON VLADINIR
I named this photo "Sweet Sexy Serenity," because this is exactly how I live my life. I live in Detroit. My wife took this at a modeling expo I was in—another passion I am pursuing. It was taken in late September downtown, in front of the Renaissance Center building. I am also an author. The title of my first book is "Surviving Both Sides." I love life and walk completely by faith.

HAMERSLY, KATHERINE ANN
This is a photo of my granddaughter, Isabella. My husband, Craig, and I love her very much. She is the best baby.

HAMILTON, KELSEY JAYE
This is a photo I took of my dad's guitar. He had just gotten a new Martin and the beautiful wood grains and textures inspired me to take a picture. I've always dreamed of pictures that are taken or painted from a perspective that is uncommon. The guitar and love of photography mixed together produced this picture. Thank God for the motivation and talent.

HAMPTON, MELISSA JEAN
We always take a few photos on the first day of school. I took a few shots of her standing and smiling with book bag in hand, but my favorites were the ones I took when she wasn't aware of the camera. The year of this photo, my daughter was starting kindergarten, but she wanted to be a first grader. She was almost old enough to make it. This year, she enjoys the fact that she skipped second grade and is now a third grader. We recently moved in with family in Oregon only to have our house burn down. Thankfully, we all have so many reasons to keep smiling. We are enjoying starting fresh and creating new memories.

HARMON, BARBARA ANN
I'm a fifty-seven-year-old housewife who loves the great outdoors and nature. I live in a small Northern California community with my husband, but I spend half my time traveling in midwestern Idaho and the Pacific Northwest. My hobbies are photography, traveling, and fishing. While staying in Riggings, Idaho, we took a side trip into a wilderness. We followed the winding Salmon River. This photograph was the perfect feeling of the day.

HARPER, WHITNEY NICOLE
My name is Whitney Harper, and photography is my passion. My quote is, "It takes a moment to capture a lifetime's worth of memories." The photo is of Dylan and Heleigh at Dylan's third birthday on September 2, 2007. He is truly loved!

HART, THOMAS W.
I am a truck driver on Vancouver Island. As I was driving south on the Old Island Highway, I came across this view. This was just after a rather severe summer storm. The location is about halfway between Courtenay and Campbell River at a place called Oyster Bay. I saw it and just knew I had to have a photo of it. Now I am pleased to be able to share its beauty.

HART, VALERIE JEAN
Trenton, my one and only child, was a six-month-old when this photograph was taken. I was doing his first photo shoot to send pictures to the family when he started fussing. My husband came home early that day, and in an effort to make Trenton happy again and finish the shoot, he picked him up and started talking and playing with him. I was going for a shot when my husband was making him laugh. At that instant, Trenton rocked back in his father's arms and gave the biggest smile he had all night. Trenton's bright eyes, big smile, and

folded hands combined for a picture of obvious love and adoration. I can't help but smile every time I see my boys in that moment I captured. Trenton's first birthday will be this April.

HATFIELD, JOSHUA DEAN
This photo was taken off of a logging road located out of Lincoln City, Oregon. I found it by accident one day and keep on going back.

HAUSER, APRIL A.
Photography has always been a hobby of mine. I am rarely in front of the camera. You will likely find me behind my camera taking the best pictures I can. One August afternoon, I was able to capture this rainbow on Lake Michigan while attending a wedding anniversary party for two of our friends. When I first saw the rainbow, it was already starting to fade. I quickly grabbed my camera to capture the shot. I think this photo shows a rainbow from a unique point of view since we rarely get to see the end of the rainbow.

HAWKINS, CORRINA PAM
This picture was taken on our annual Easter holiday. It was our first Easter holiday since our fifteen-year-old son, Michael, was killed. Apart from being uniquely Australian, like Michael, watching and capturing this sunset brought me some comfort, as I believe it shows peace and tranquility. It's a place Michael loved to go and it means so much that this picture has been chosen for publication. Michael's sisters, Jessica and Alison, will be able to cherish this photo for years to come as a peaceful reminder of the beloved brother's favorite annual Easter holiday.

HAYES, LOUISE
"Bird Of Paradise" was taken in my parents' garden. It was my first time using slide film. I love sharing my photos with friends and family, and I love taking photos of them, especially my two children, Michellie and Aston. I would like to say thank you to my family and friends for encouraging me with my photography. Thank you for allowing me to explore my gift from God. May it take us places we could never dream.

HENDERSON, MICHELLE ANN
Thanks to my two-year-old colt, Echo, this photo reminds me to pause and enjoy the sunset. I've had Echo since he was ten hours old, or should I say, he had me. He captured my heart and I've taken hundreds of photos as he has grown.

HERTEL, TIFFANY LAZETTE
I have a nice sized pothole in my driveway. I decided to fill it up with water and see what would happen if someone jumped in it. My cousin was over and I asked her to jump into the pothole. I was amazed at how well it turned out, so I continued to shoot at different angles. Experimenting in photography is a great lesson because you learn so much from your successes and your mistakes.

HOETS, LEIGH-ANN CHASE
Growing up in South Africa has provided me with a passion for wildlife and photography. This photograph of an impala lily was taken at one of my favorite places, Tiger Bay, or Lake Kariba in Zimbabwe. I am delighted to share this picture of

one of the most beautiful pieces of wildlife in the African bush.

HOPPA, BRITTNEY

Being twenty years old and majoring in digital film making and video at the Illinois Institute of Art in Schaumburg, photography has always been a huge interest of mine. I have always tried to take a creative edge on my photos when using my camera. This photo is of my one-year-old puppy, Coco. Because she is a huge diva, she loves her picture taken.

HOSTETLER, DIANE KAY

When I look at this photo, I can hear the waves beating on the shore, feel the warm sand on my feet, and hear the breeze through the trees. That trip was an amazing time. It will forever remind me of that peaceful walk I had with a friend that day. I am a photographer, inside and out. Making it a business for me is not as exciting as just taking pictures. It's how I see the world and how the world sees me. There are so many times I could take the moment in life I just experienced and put it on paper. I graduated from Milligan College with a bachelor's degree and now live the life of a struggling artist. Thanks to those who have helped, inspired, and influenced me throughout my years so far on Earth.

HOWARD, ADAM N.

Adam Howard is a four-time Emmy-Award winning visual effects supervisor living in San Francisco, California.

HUGHES, GEORGIA KAY

This photo was taken at Twin Rocks, Oregon. Traveling and seeing new sites is a delight of mine. I was the sole person on the beach that morning and had taken several pictures at this location. I was walking back to my car when I decided to turn and take one more photo. Remembering this scene—the solitude of the beach, the serenity from the sky, and the power of the waves will fill my soul from now on.

HUNLIN, SHELLEY ANN

I found that photography was my gift at eight years old and have been taking pictures continously wherever the road takes me. I find taking pictures of nature is magical. It takes me into my own element, and I experience happiness in letting other people know how important nature is!

HURD, JESSICA LYNN

I've never been a photography fanatic; however, I have always had an eye for a great photograph. I titled this picture "Canvas Hands," because, like a painted canvas, each girl has a meaningful story behind the writing on her hand. It means so much to me that I was able to capture so many stories in only one frame.

IBRAGIMOV, JAQUELINE

I like to spend quality time with my mom, Yana, on the weekends and during our vacation time. We used to photograph each other a lot. One day in August 2007, at the end of my summer break, I suddenly became bored and she gave me a camera to run around with in the garden and take as many pictures as I liked. I have taken thousands of pic-

tures of nature, and now I can't stop. A whole new world has opened up for me.

ILIYN, DAVID JAMES

In July of 2007 when I was fifteen years old, my dad and I traveled to five southern Africa countries. I was just learning to use my new camera. We were staying at a game farm in Zimbabwe and when I woke in the morning, I was stunned to see wild animals roaming freely. There were two four-month-old sibling lion cubs that seemed to have free reign to roam the premises. They were so cute, playful, and very expressive. I took lots of pictures and this was one of my favorites.

IVANOSKOS, PAULA TERESE

Last summer, while camping at Clearwater Lake in Meredith, North Hampshire with my family, the picture, "Serenity," was born. It was the perfect day, the sun was shining and the lake was crystal clear. The other subjects I love to photograph are my beloved pets, Golden, the yellow Labrador, and two cats, Callie and Lucy. My husband, Bob, and I have three boys, Ryan, Andrew, and Michael. Working as a nurse can be hectic at times, so I love to balance out my life with photography. I have other hobbies as well, like knitting, reading, writing and attending my sons' basketball and baseball games.

IVELJA, JULIANA LUCIA

A Sydney-based artist, Juliana completed her diploma of fine arts in 2007, majoring in photography and painting. She is an expressive artist bringing life to her work. Juliana exhibits quite regularly and her works consist of mediums such as photography, oils, acrylics, and mixed media. Inspired by Andre Kertesz, "Memory" is a series of nine images of her family in which glass and light were used, a key to reliving the past. The photos were taken while on holiday at Maloneys Beach on the Southern Coast of Australia, a place which has come to be an inspiration for many of her works.

JACKSON, SUSAN D.

This is the very first photo I snapped of Dozer upon his arrival at our home. My husband and I had been adopted by him only a few hours earlier, so to see him looking so happy and excited while he was checking out his new surroundings made us feel good. I knew it was a memory in the making and that I had better get the camera and take a photo. He has been a happy and exciting blessing in our lives every day since!

JACOBS, ALICIA MARIE

I was visiting Paris, France for three days. When we first arrived, it was gloomy and raining nonstop. Thankfully, the next day, it stopped. I woke up to a sunny day and went seeing the sights. This setting caught my eye. The blue, cloudy sky and green trees made my picture beautiful. I am lucky to have had the chance to capture such an amazingly breathtaking picture.

JACOBS, EMILY RUTH

This is a photo of my two-year-old New Foundland, Felony. I had just gotten home for Thanksgiving break and he was laying on the porch. I never thought this would turn out as well

as it did. This just proves that you never know how good or bad something will turn out, so take everything you can.

JEFFRIES, BETH R.

The sky represents life; continuously moving, forever-changing, and at the same time, beautiful and priceless. So often, people take for granted the surroundings God has created. So many people are in search of new forms of art, but what they fail to realize is that every day they witness the timeless masterpiece of the one true artist, God.

JENKINS, BENNIE P.

This is a photo of Sparkal the clown entertaining children. She has the look of excitement and laughter in this photo. Her laugh is so big I can see her tonsils. Sparkal is sparkling with laughter. I like clowns—clowns make people happy. Sparkal is doing a good job and this expression was fun to capture. I have taken lots of pictures, but this one stole my heart. A smile is the heart of a clown. Smile!

JENKINS, TARA

Some mornings you wake up to unexpected surprises. October 2007 in Castor, Alberta it was just that—an unexpected beauty with the sun rising. My ten-minute drive to town took thirty-five, I couldn't put the camera down.

JENSEN, SHERRON SWAPP

My pug, Marley, is a ham when a camera is pointed at him. During a Christmas shoot, I grabbed my son's glasses and Marley took such a delight in posing. This one just stole my heart, and my Aussie friend named it right. I take pictures of a variety of subjects ready for framing and using for home decor and fun animal shots.

JOBSON, JODY LYNN

My photo, "Night Lily," sparked my interest in photography. I had just recently purchased a new camera and was taking pictures of everything. The tiger lily in the picture is one of the flowers in my mom's flower beds, and is one of my favorites. I took it at night and I was very pleased with the way it turned out. Since then, I have being doing some portraits for family and friends, as well as looking into taking photography further.

JOCA, TAMI A.

I have always been told to take time and to stop to smell the roses. This never applied to me. I am a workaholic by nature, and I was busy getting my website running. My puppy whined to go outside. After he was finished, Rowdy plopped down on the deck just outside of the house and stared up at me as if telling me to stop and play. Time seemed still as I looked at that cute little puppy. Rowdy is much larger now, but I will never forget that look on that day.

JOHANSEN, BELINDA JANE

This is a photo of my son, James, aged six years. He looked so at peace while sleeping on this particular night that I couldn't resist taking this photograph of him. I have four children—James and triplet daughters, Maggie, Grace, and Emma. Through clicking away to capture my children's milestones, I found a love of photography.

JOHNSGAARD, BRAILYN TYRELL

This photo was taken out on the water at the Saskatchewan Landing in my dad's fancy new boat. One evening, I decided to go out on the bow of the boat to get a picture of the sunset. After taking many pictures, while trying to keep my balance on the swiftly moving boat, I captured a few shots that I really liked. I have also taken many other photos like this one. Some of my hobbies are playing guitar with my band, and taking agricultural and scenic pictures on our Saskatchewan farm. I take my camera almost everywhere I go. You never know when you might come across something that requires something more than just a snapshot in your mind. This photo is definitely a keeper.

JOHNSON, COREY D.

My name is Corey Johnson. I'm a singer/songwriter and my stage name is "Musicorey" because I love music so much. I've always wanted to be a model, actor, and a recording artist.

JOHNSON, DON ROY

This was taken on a backpack trip along the West Highland Way between Glasgow and Fort William, Scotland. I try to have a camera ready at all times on a walk, because you just never know what you might see. The walk is ninety-five miles long and took me four days to complete. I was very suprised, as this was the first photo I have ever entered into a contest.

JOHNSON, JOANN

Ernie, my husband, and I continually look for scenic photo opportunities. We relocated to Illinois, in late 2005. In winter 2006 a very large ice storm passed through. The property we bought has a small fruit tree orchard of about twenty trees. The photo is of two of them. We caught the sunlight reflecting off the branches and through the ice early that evening and knew this would make a great photo. "Ice Storm" is just one of the photos taken that day. We hope you enjoy it as much as we do.

JOHNSON, MARVIN E.

My daughters, Diana and Valarie, came running to me telling me that Boots was using the bathroom. As luck would have it, my camera was ready, so I grabbed it and got this shot.

JOHNSON, RYAN HARRISON

I love playing music and taking photos. This photo is a reflection of that. It combines art and music. I think they both go hand in hand, which is what I wanted to capture.

JOHNSON-GARRARD, DESIREE STAR

Harold and I were on our honeymoon in July 2007 at Cherokee, North Carolina, when we saw this unique bear. Harold was feeding it over the top of the highest wall and chainlink fence. We thought this was the most dangerous bear there. As Harold was feeding him, I told the bear to pose for the camera. That was when the bear laid flat on his back and started moving around and it appeared that he was dancing. Harold and I looked at each other and said, "That bear definitely knows how to get what he wants."

JOHNSTON, STEVE MARTIN

Joy is something not all of us are able to to do on our own. If I can capture images of our natural world to share the feeling of a serene morning in the Canadian Rockies, or any of the marvels of nature, then I have shared some of the best in my world with the rest of you.

JONES, ANDRE

I love the fall season, I think it's the most colorful time of the year. God reveals His palette of color and puts us in awe. One early November morning, I left my home to run an errand. Driving along, I noticed this tree and thought, "My God, that's beautiful!" I immediately circled the block, parked my car, and walked around this tree. The color was just breathtaking! I walked around, looking through my view-finder for the angle that would give me what I saw—that wonderful color. This photo was taken in the early morning, approximately 9:43 a.m. I used a Panasonic DMC FZ-30 digital camera.

JONES, BRENDA KAY

I've often heard it said, "You don't pick the horse, the horse picks you," and this was so true of my Pasofino, Rett, though I was sad that I was not the recipient of his love—it became obvious that Lacy was. After seeing their interaction together while on a ride in Hoston Woods, where this beautiful photograph, "Love," was taken, I knew they belonged together. After running free in a field for four years, Rett came out of retirement, and with the love they had for each other, took first place in their 4-H class in Preble County, Ohio.

JONES, GAYNOR

I love photographing animals! I find their individual features as fascinating as the animals themselves. I started by taking pictures of my pets. I did some experimenting, taking close-ups of their noses, feet, ears, etc. I loved how the photos came out and now it's one of my favorite ways to photograph animals!

JONES, STEPHANIE LYDIE

This is a picture of my son, Jeremy, also known as Bubba, who just happened to look so beautiful and content just standing around, watching the birds fly around him. He was my inspiration for this photograph, as he is for everything else I do in my life. This is dedicated to my beautiful little angel boy. Mommy loves you.

JONES, STEVE

This is the Golden Buddha at Chiang Saen, North Thailand. Sitting along the Mekong River, this statue was built in 2004 to replace an earlier one lost in a flood. It stands fifteen meters high and ten meters wide, tipping the scales at sixty-nine tons. The picture was taken using a Sony DSC-P9, then removing the noise using neat image software. A big thanks to my wife, Sairung, who came from the nearby village of Mae Chan.

JORDAN, JULIE ANNE

A fifteen-month deployment is hard. I took this picture when my husband was in Iraq. As lonely as I was, I still found beauty in my front yard.

JOSEPH, STEFANIE A.

I believe that photography is something that runs in my blood. For as long as I can remember, my dad has always been behind the camera. It is the thing we have in common that we both love. I took this photograph at my high school's fair of a mother and her children getting food at a stand. Just the way the children and mother were interacting was captivating to me. A moment like that can convey so many emotions. I am very happy that I had my camera on me, because you never know when a moment and amazing shot like this will come along.

JUNG, KUMSEOK

Freedom of interpretation is the greatest part of art. But it's not like we have to interpret, is it?

KARN, JAYMIE SILKEN

Photography isn't my usual artistic medium, but it's definitely becoming one of my favorites. I was on vacation with my family and we decided to stop in Quebec for the night. Just before sunset, everything outside of our hotel was kissed with an amazing glow. "Look On The Bright Side" is just one of many photos that I took that evening. I am very proud of this piece and am ecstatic that it's now published.

KARN, WESLEY ADAM

This picture was taken from Indian Head on Fraser Island in Australia, where I spent three days and two very cold nights. We did not bring enough warm clothing with us for that trip to Fraser Island during a three-month adventure in Australia. The Sandbar Island is incredibly beautiful, as is the rest of the country. It's difficult to write only one hundred words about a picture when it's worth one thousand. I hope you enjoy my photograph.

KARPINSKI, CHARLES HENRY

I wanted to compose and present a scene in life that showed the unity of the subjects almost mystically blending into one. I enjoy the simplicity of it, underscoring the strong and powerful universal human image it creates. Also, it reflects the sanctity of the theme in respect to the title. This is in memory of my wife, Yvonne, who passed away recently. This particular image was found in her own personal, private photo collection of selected ones that I had taken of her over the years, which I was cataloguing and processing.

KEARSE, CYNDI ANN

This is a picture of my daughter and my mother who was undergoing chemotherapy for lung cancer. Through the seventeen-month ordeal, she never lost her sense of humor. She died eight months after this picture was taken. This was submitted in honor of her courageous fight.

KELLEY, SHARON LYNN

Having tried in my home for thirty-nine years now, this was the first time I have had hummingbirds, and oddly enough, it was the dead of winter. I ran to get them some nectar, and this is what I got, "Ruby Tuesday," a total redhead. God has blessed me.

KELLY, SHANNAN

Here are the two loves of my life. As I sat on the beach behind them, I felt the need to capture this special moment between father and daughter. This is the first time our daughter, Kaylana, had been to the lake. It was so beautiful that day, the water was so sparkling clean and the sky was so blue and clear. The view of the snow-tipped mountaintops and the serenity that surrounded the area will remain in my memory as a beautiful moment with my beautiful family.

KENDRICK, JENNA M.

I came from a large circle of shutterbugs and seeing the photos my family captured has intrigued me to continue taking snapshots wherever I go. I reside in Massachusetts on a family farm with my two daughters, Kylie and Casey. I love to watch my girls grow and see life as they do, simple. My youth spent in Minnesota led me to take photos of still life and scenery. Human interactions when no one's looking strike my curiosity; some of life's precious moments are depicted here. I will always cherish this photo of Casey and her first play date with Autumn.

KENNEDY, KAYLIN KRYSTAL

Born and raised in small Minot, North Dakota, where there really isn't anything to do, I found a hobby in taking pictures. It wasn't until 2006, the year my son, Ian, was born, that I turned my simple hobby into a passion, simply out of the love for my son and for photography. I found that the most precious of photos are the ones that are unposed. They immediately touch all those who see them and leave imprints on my heart.

KENNY, MICHAEL DAVID

This photograph was taken during a hike off the beaten path high up in the Canadian Rockies when my friend stopped to take a breather. I saw him up above amidst this spectacular scenery and had to take a picture—I'm glad I did! This photograph represents my passion, the mountains. They are my domain—a place where freedom is felt and limits are pushed.

KENT, HANNAH REBEKAH

"Dry Shadows" is a photo of a barn located in our neighborhood. I thought the bare tree limbs shadows gave extra character to the hundred-year-old barn. I love to take pictures of almost everything, so I almost always have a camera with me. People, places, and things are all suitable subjects, especially in spontaneous photos.

KIDD, SAMANTHA BRITTANY

This is a picture I took at a butterfly conservatory in Cambridge, Ontario in the summer of 2007. I am currently a student about to study my passion for photography at Humber College. Special thanks to my family, and best friend, Jessica, for all the support!

KIDD, TOSHA ANN

I'm seventeen years old and a senior in high school. I'm seldom, if ever, without my camera. My friends call me "The Camera Queen." I was on a hiking trip when I saw this amazing reflection in a shallow bed of water. I thought it would make a beautiful nature shot—a pretty water bed reflecting the overhanging rocks above. Two pictures with just one click.

KINIRY, DEBI J.

I had met up with family in Pennsylvania for a surprise birthday party this past fall. My niece planned the entire weekend and part of the plan was a picnic at a beautiful park. You couldn't have asked for a better day for October to have a picnic and take pictures. We all had our cameras out that day. The foliage, the sun, and perfectly crisp air made for a great day, and this is one of the results of that day.

KIVELL, ASHLEE AMANDA

I am just an amateur photographer looking to make a career out of a hobby. After purchasing my first digital SLR just last year, it has never left my hands. One gloomy morning my roommate, Sarah, was peering out the sliding glass doors of our eighth-floor apartment. When I glanced over at her, she was merely a silhouette against the foggy glass. I immediately told her to hold it and snapped the picture. Once the shutter clicked, I knew I had captured something special.

KNOBLAUCH, KRISTI ANN

This is my photo of my niece, Mallorie. The picture explains how I see her. When I look at her, I just detatch from everything surrounding her and that's why I used the black-and-white effect. She is my favorite thing to photograph.

KOSTER, PETER

On a Sunday afternoon in fall of 2007, I was driving on III Avenue, heading west, and saw on the left a golden hue, so I went around the block and parked there. The midday sun was shining brightly and I stepped out of the car in amazement and took two pictures, and I zoomed in to get a closer look at the second one. This picture is not only my favorite, but many others' too.

KOYNE, CAROL J.

Considered an amateur photographer since grade school, I enjoy snapping impromptu photos of the unexpected. My first camera was a Brownie camera in which the film was manually wound from picture to picture and had no flash attachment. Now when I take pictures, I look for the unusual and that which will stimulate the imagination. I am intrigued by water fowl and their antics. This picture, "Dancing In The Park," was taken as the geese crossed the street in the park on their way to the ponds. I was elated and felt privileged to be given this fascinating graceful, bird show.

KOZAK, CARY

The word "mainstream" blows through the wind. We hear the echoes on the parkway and pitch increases on our interstates. Much like the parachutes from the pappus of a wished-upon dandelion, our dreams tend to be lost in this mainstream environment. The constants in society tend to dwindle on and disintegrate one's insight on life. "Red Wash Out" is an example of stopping to record a moment in time. Not only is the image itself meaningful, but the events that occur before and after are just as important.

KRUEGER, TIMOTHY C.

Chicago actor Tim Krueger takes an energizing, deep-breathing, sun-gazing walk along the shores of Lake Michigan five or six days a week at sunrise, always with his camera. The "Chicago Sunrise" picture was taken during one of these walks in December 2007, while standing near the entrance to Montrose Harbor. The Hancock Tower can be seen in the distance.

KRUSE, DEBORAH A.

I have loved photography since I can remember. I love taking photos of nature, horses, people, concerts, and auto racing—like I said, I love photography. I took this photo one morning in October of 2005 out on my patio—I couldn't believe my eyes. I took a whole series of them as the sky changed. I still am amazed by them. I get an amazing amount of pleasure when other people enjoy my photographs.

KUNKEL, PAUL CHRIS

I had just recently gotten back into photography in December 2006. My wife and I were on an eight-mile walk in November 2007. Still carrying my Nikon D70 everywhere I go, we came across this absolutely gorgeous meadow and with the help of a park bench and my circular polarizer, this picture was born. I think the farmer put the bench there just to look at his meadow.

KUNSTEK, LOUIS WILLIAM

This magnificent bird is one of nature's great hunters and totally trainable, but never quite domesticated. My neighbors have tried to feed and befriend him. He prefers to pick and choose from the abundant wildlife here in Florida. This camera has never zoomed in so clearly.

KYLE, ELIZABETH S.

This is a photo of my oldest, Patrick, and my youngest, Claudia, at their brother, Alex's, soccer game. We were living in the Middle East and they played soccer at the American school there. This is just one of the many fond memories of living there. We take lots of photos of our children and looking at them is one of our favorite pastimes.

LA BRUYERE, J. P. EDWARD

This tragic scene of "La Pobre Vieja," which is Spanish for "the poor old woman," was captured before the gothic cathedral in Burgos, Spain. I was fortunate enough to venture on a tour throughout Spain on a school trip when I was sixteen years old. I feel this honor is undeserved as I profit from the misfortune of others, but I am glad that with this piece, I may spread awareness to the issue of poverty. On that same trip, I was given some very inspiring words by a street performer, "El arte no es realidad, aqui todo puede ser," or "Art is not reality; here, all can be."

LACROIX, PATRICK

I've been passionate about photography for a very long time. I love the region where I live, Mauricie, for its wildlife. I took this photo of a marsh in "La Cite de L'Energie," in Shawinigan. I had just prepared to phtograph when this frog jumped in front of me, as if it wanted to know why I was there. Fortunately, my finger was fast enough to freeze this extraordinary moment.

LAWRENCE, MALLORY RAE
I'm from Burbank, California, and I've always loved cruising down the 101. My mom and I were coming back home from San Diego with the top down and the wind blowing in our hair. I wanted to capture a piece of the freeway in Los Angeles that didn't make the city look like the polluted area it is often potrayed as.

LAYNG, SIMON JAMES
This is a photo of the scene outside the road construction camp. I was working at in Baker Lake, Nunavert. The early morning sun was peering through a thick fog that created the surreal atmosphere, which I was lucky enough to capture on film. I am a remote caterer working in the Canadian Arctic, a job which provides many good photo opportunities.

LEAL, DARLEEN
This is a photo of Max Leal, my Boxer, running past me at the beach smiling as if he was saying, "Hey, there!"

LEE, GODWINE
Taken in October 2007, this picture of Tokyo, Japan reflects the livelihood of the city. My initial plan was to name this "The Gale Of Hope," as my first impression was, "In darkness, a path shall light itself."

LEISERSON, DAVID AVERY
This was taken in the first week of January, 2006. I wasn't nearly as much of a photo nerd as I am now, but I had gotten my camera for that exact reason; immortalizing those priceless moments with family and friends. In the photo, my brother, Ken, and his wife, Heidi, are watching the sunset across San Francisco Bay at the Lawrence Hall of Science in Berkely.

LEMONS, DARRIN
This photograph was taken on a family trip to Sea World in Orlando, Florida. My stepson loves killer whales, so we went to see Shamu. Imagine the wonder in his eyes when he saw Shamu flying out of the water.

LEON, MISCHA D.
This is a photograph that was taken in front of the house in my parents' garden. It is just one of many flowers that they so proudly grow and display during the spring and summer seasons. What is unique about the flower in this picture is the way the sun strikes the flower and makes it appear as a radiant star; that is why I decided to give it the title "Garden Delight."

LEWALLEN, MEGAN MARIE
Photography has been a passion of mine for quite some time and I have found that more often than not, I am drawn to nature over any other subject. Also, for as young as I am, I have had the opportunity to visit some truly beautiful places around the world. The chance to capture photos in countries such as Australia and New Zealand have left me with many beautiful shots. However, this photo taken nearly two years ago at Niagara Falls is definitely one of my favorites.

LILLY, RACHEL RANDALL
My son was two weeks old in this photograph. He just looked so thoughtful and sweet, I just had to have this picture. The child in this photograph is Dakota, son of Tray and Rachel Lilly.

LIMBAUGH, DELACEY AMBER
This is a photo of my eye. It was one of the first pictures I took with my FinePix Fujifilm S700. I've been involved with photography for about a year now. I also like painting, drawing, and listening to music.

LITOURNEAU, THERESA E.
This is my six-month-old Standard Poodle. She is extremely bright, active, and often inscrutible. Incredibly charming, her spirit constantly draws me into the mystery and joy of living with another species. The depth of this is captured here, in her eyes, and they always draw me in.

LLOYD, ARTHUR CHRISTOPHER
This photograph was captured during a moment of awe. When I stumbled upon this breathtaking view off the coast of the Pacific Ocean in Washington state, I had no choice but to capture it on film.

LONG, ABIGAIL MARIE
This picture was taken on a trip I took to Spain in 2007. This picture only shows a fraction of what the little town of Toledo is really like. Until then, I really wasn't sure a place like that even existed. I hope to go back one day. Though the picture is nice, there is nothing like seeing it with your own eyes and not from behind a lens.

LONG, SANDY NANOD
This sunset was captured on my favorite beach in Hawaii, on the island of Oahu, located in Makaha called Keawa'ula, locally known as "Yokes."

LOPARDO, KAROLINE
In late summer of 2007, I found myself driving by a small grove of sunflowers every evening on my way home from work. One day, I finally pulled over to look at them closely. I took several photos; each flower was unique in its own way. However, this photo immediately became my favorite. This somewhat small sunflower, not yet in bloom, stood apart from all the others. Although it is not showy and colorful, its still beautiful in my eyes. This photograph is now one of my favorites. It is one of the best photos I have ever taken.

LOVEJOY-WELCH, BARBARA JEAN
I am no photographer, just a proud mom. This picture was taken in 1993, when all three came home for Christmas. They are the third generation of military men. Carl was in the air force, Michael was in the army's 82nd Airborne, and Wayne was in the Coast Guard. They were all named after their grandfather, Carl Lovejoy, or their father, Miles Wayne Welch.

LY, MIKE
This is a photograph of my adorable son, Tevin, watching outdoor rock climbing at the Fairfax County Fair. Tevin is the first grandchild on both sides of the family, and he was two years old when the picture was taken. This phototgraph was taken from my camera phone and I'm surprised at how well the picture turned out. I captured this photograph because the look of focus and the expression on his face put a smile on my face when I saw it. It was a moment to cherish and hold on to, so I wanted to keep this memory forever. Daddy loves you, Tevin!

LYLES, HARRY TROISE
I took this photo in Florence, Italy, in July 2007. The museums and churches were beautiful, but it was this common, urban view that caught my eye.

LYMAN, JENNIFER
I am a senior photography student of Fitchburg State College and over the summer in 2007, I studied abroad in Italy. Through my travels around the country, I was fulfilling many photography assignments. "Venetian Way" was the product of a reflection assignment in Venice. The idea was to catch a reflection that did not obviously depict Venice, but to show Venice in a subtle way. So I hopped onto a gondola and shot this photo when we were coming around a corner. I was able to crop enough of the building out so that it was not obvious where the photo was taken, and I left the reflection in the water to represent the unique beauty of the Venetian waterway.

LYONS, HAJNALKA TIMEA
I was living in England and some friends and I decided to take our first road trip to Wales. We went to visit one of my old school friends from Hungary. The weather was beautiful all day, but when we were ready to go to the beach, it became extremely cold. We celebrated the last day of the summer with barbeque and fireworks. The next day, my friend showed us around, and we visited many breathtaking places. We stopped on the side of the road because we couldn't resist this field with this beautiful view. Whenever I look at this photo it reminds me of that road trip to Wales.

MACDOUGALL, MARY DORIS
I have loved taking snapshots since I was a child. I love to take nature pictures and pictures of animals mostly, but also of babies and children. I usually have my camera with me and love to capture random shots. I am the mother of twelve children, thirty grandchildren and twenty great-grandchildren. I live in Hudique, Cape Breton, and I was driving home from Port Hawkesbury when I captured this sunset. Creignish, Cape Breton is a wonderful place to capture beautiful pictures.

MARIE, RITA J.
This was probably one of the most exciting and frightening pictures I have ever taken. It's of one of the biggest storms in the Carolinas—gale winds and monstrous waves. The only way I could get the shot was to go out to the end of the dock, about fifty feet out, with the wind blowing me around a bit, but there it was, a twenty-foot wave cresting absolutely beautifully! I had never seen anything so magnificent—the true power of the ocean! It was a crazy thing to do, but I would do it again in a heartbeat!

MARRIS-WALKER, JENNIFER K.
This photograph, entitled "King Of The Hill," was

taken in Ontario, Canada in August 2007. It showcases a male scimitar-horned oryx, contently perched atop his manmade mountain facility at a local wildlife conservatory. My two great passions in life are travel and photography. I believe that travel broadens one's view and understanding of the world. As an artist, I seek only to document my own personal experiences, to capture events and scenes as I see them, and to share with others the beauty and diversity of the world I've seen.

MARSH, TOM C.

I was walking through the woods after a typical winter's day, and came across this tree that was different from all the other trees in the area. I thought that it would make a great photo with the strip of snow on the bark, so I shot the photo thinking that it was kind of cool. Then I got real close and took this shot. I am just an ordinary guy who looks at life as a journey. If I can freeze a moment in time to get a real look at something or someone, that is great. That moment in time that you freeze through a photo will never change in this ever-changing world.

MARSHALL, FREDERICK

This is a photo of my flowers my wife created for my eightieth birthday party. I will be eighty-four in July 2008 and still play tennis three times a week. Photography is my hobby and I recently attended a course on photography. I was the chairman of an engineering company that manufactured machinery for the plastic industry.

MARTIN, LISA RENA'

This is a photo of our dog, Bo. I wanted a unique photo for my Christmas cards and this was it! Bo wasn't very excited about the process, but after several attempts of adjusting poses and coaxing with doggie treats, I captured the perfect photo for my cards. The expression on his face says it all. I wonder what he was really thinking! I love to take photos of any subject. When I look through the lens of my camera, I know there is no limit to what I will discover.

MARTINEZ, EVA

This is a photo of my son, Ismael, that I used as a Christmas greeting card. My precious baby was diagnosed with asthma when he was born and has been a fighter since. The first year was very tough; I was constantly out of work to take him to the doctor and even surgeons. Ismael was always sick—they even removed his tonsils and placed tubes in his ears. Throughout these couple of years, he has beaten his asthma. It has been over a year and half and he still has not been back to the doctors. Ismael is a fighter and is a very smart and handsome boy. Ismael loves to play his guitar, drums, keyboard, and loves to sing. Ismael's dad is a singer in a Latin band named Grupo Misterio. Ismael is following in his dad's footsteps. Ismael has an older brother named Manual that he loves dearly. I, Eva Martinez, am a proud parent of two children, Ismael Saucedo and Manual Huerta.

MARTINEZ, MARITZA BARBARA

I was born in Palma Soriano, Santiago de Cuba. I reside with my family in Miami, Florida, and I have a bachelor's degree in Spanish. My hobbies are music, reading, and taking pictures of friends,

family, and landscapes. "Atardecer En El Sur De Tenerife" was taken in November of 2002. I took the picture because I was impacted by its natural beauty. The landscape of the place impacted me, and the dusk is shown with black and red tones in that heavenly southern place of Tenerife.

MATHIAS, NATASHA MELISSA

I live in a remote area on Ababika Lake in a little cabin in the woods. I love taking pictures of nature and wildlife. I feel it's a rare opportunity to catch a moment in time like this, I feel so lucky to have captured something so amazing for a beginner with her first camera. I hope that people see this rare beauty and want to protect the eagles' natural environment from being destroyed.

MAZO, MICHAEL LEE

Hope is what I see in this little girl's eyes. She lives in a village south of Ensenapa, British Columbia in a town called El Zorrillo. We support a church there by bringing food, building houses, and offering spiritual support. When she received a new blanket for the winter, I saw hope in her.

McCLELLAND, DAWN ANGELA

I'm twenty-seven years old and I was born and raised in the West Midlands before moving to Blackpool in 2005. I took this photo on a day trip to Manchester. I started out looking at the different architectural styles found in the city center when I came across these pigeons. I found it quite comical as they seemed to be having a business meeting over lunch, just as we humans do. What is a waste to us is a banquet to them!

McCOY, BRADLEY DERRING

As far back as I can remember, I've enjoyed outdoor activities. When I got older, around age eight, I was given the family Polaroid camera. It was then that I first discovered photography. Ever since, I've become more and more interested in taking better shots. My favorites include sunsets like the one I submitted, but also clouds from a blue sky or one about to show us the power of a thunderstorm. I also enjoy sports photography, but nothing will ever take first place over our world and the endless beauty it possesses.

McKOWN, SAMANTHA EILEEN

This photo was taken on one of the beaches in Juneau, Alaska. It is about the middle of June 2007. Brooke is my middle child and my sneaky one. We were looking for shells and I was taking pictures of everyone. Well, I looked over at Brooke and she looked like she was doing something she shouldn't be. I yelled at her, "What are you doing?" and as she looked up, I had to take her picture because kids make the cutest faces when you catch them off guard. She wasn't doing anything but digging in the sand. Brooke is one-and-a-half years old.

McLAIN, DONALD J.

Eleven family members went on a hike. Ten of them took this picture of my three-year-old granddaughter taking our group picture.

McNAUGHTON, JENNIFER

I have been taking photographs since I was eleven

years old. My favourite subjects are pets and wildlife, landscapes, and people of all ages, shapes, and sizes. This is a photograph of my Alaskan Malamute, Aurora, crunching on an icicle. She is a rescued dog from the Alaskan Malamute Help League in Canada. I deliberately moved in low and close to offer this unique view.

McNEAL, WILLIE

When I took this picture, this is what I saw. The weather-battered face of an old man, the face of a young girl dressed in a white sweater and black pants, standing next to a white shaggy dog.

MELLEN, YAHSHA TAMIDAH

This is a photo of my niece. We were outside in the front yard playing around and taking pictures and she just turned around right as I photographed her, and I wasn't expecting it to come out so great. I guess you can say I'm a picture freak, but it's worth it. Having this picture in this book really means a lot to my family, but the one who is really proud is my dad. He saw this and his eyes lit up. There wasn't a star in the sky that shined brighter than his eyes.

MENDELEVICH, ELENA

This is a photo of my daughter, Sophie Michelle. I took this photo when Sophie was just one month old. She likes to make cute faces, so I try to have my camera with me at all times to capture these priceless moments.

MESSER, DIANE

I took this picture at Gulf Breeze Zoo. Every year they have Zoo Lights in celebration of Christmas. The children were so excited, and when Toni Leigh saw the petting zoo with all the animals, she squealed with delight and right about that time, the goat stuck its head out of the fence like he was looking for a kiss and Toni Leigh obliged.

METCALF, MICHAEL BRYAN

This photo is one of several taken from the colonnade atop St. Isaac's Cathedral in St. Petersburg, Russia. I was there in June 2006 on a study-abroad trip. My photography class went to St. Isaac's during an all-night field trip, which is when this photo was taken.

MIELKE, JO ANNE

What a pleasant surprise to know that my fur baby, Sam Siam, has become a celebrity and has the great honor of appearing in your book. Thank you very much from Sam Siam. I am sure he will think he looks "purrfect!"

MILEVSKIY, TREVOR JOHN

After a snowstorm, I was out walking and came across this image. I thought the snow on the branches made a beautiful pattern. I enjoy the beauty that nature can present and to capture it is even better.

MILLER, CAROLE A.

Breena's picture captures the true unconditional love that we have so enjoyed with being a pet-loving family. Having English Setters for over thirty years and endless pictures of all of our loving pets, we are so honored to share Breena and in loving memories of our beloved setters.

MILLIKEN, BRIAN JAMES

I took this photo while on a camping trip with my family. I like this photo because of the way the posts on the dock line up with the river. I am a recent graduate of Rensselaer Polytechnic Institute, where I studied mechanical engineering, and now work as a design engineer for a printing press manufacturer. In my exploration of photography, I enjoy experimenting with perspectives and angles. My photographs are typically of static landscapes, though I have taken some excellent action photos at the local speedway.

MILLS, DESTINY L.

This is a photo of my sister at the river. We went to the river to hang out and play with the camera. I never intended on it turning out to be anything. We were just having fun. It was taken at the end of the day, right before we packed everything up and headed home. That's why I named the photo "The End Of A Summer Day."

MODRZAKOWSKI, ALISSA MARIE

This photo was taken in Cabo San Lucas, Mexico on the last day of a seven-day cruise. I had just received a new camera and was testing it out when the sunset became the most beautiful one I had seen the whole trip. I love this photo because of the way the clouds are lit by the sun, and the rays stream out from underneath. I grew up in Hadley, Massachusetts with a passion for photography that I hope to turn into a career someday.

MOELLER, KAITLYN DAVIS

This photograph features Megan Peppmuller, a very good friend of mine, and depicts a story meant to affect each viewer differently. Being a junior in high school, my education of photography is still in its infancy. At this point my photographs are merely a hobby, one that I do not just enjoy, but have a passion for. I specialize in concert photography, but cherish all the wonderful photographic forms.

MONAGHAN, MIKE JAMES

This is one of the first pictures I took with my newly purchased camera. All I was really doing was experimenting with it around my yard. I noticed one of our sunflowers was bigger and much healthier looking than the others. So I started snapping photographs from many different angles. When I finally got this shot, I was so proud of myself, and when people began to tell me how much they liked it, I was inspired to pursue a photography dream!

MONGAN, TRACI KAYE

This is a photo of a friend of mine and her new baby girl. I took this photo because it's not very often you see pictures in this point of view, and it also shows the love of the mother and her new baby. This is just one of many more of that day!

MONHEIM, ALLY MARIE

I took this picture, "The Trenches," on a rainy Friday night during the Orrville Red Riders versus Wooster Generals football game. The rivalry between the two high schools has been alive for over 100 years. Each game is played with great intensity and pride. This particular game had a very special meaning. Earlier in the week, one of our Red Rider football players was diagnosed with leukemia. As you can see both teams came together and wore the number 52 on their helmets despite the bitter rivalry.

MONTGOMERY, DEBORAH ANN

In front of my parents' townhome is a concrete pond. Many species of water fowl have chosen it to migrate to during the winter months, as Corpus Christi, Texas stays pretty warm. This beauty came up to me when I was visiting, asking for a snack. This photo is precious to me because both of my parents are gone now and "The Black Swan" is a happy memorial! I try to keep my camera with me at all times because you never know when or where a good photo opportunity will occur. I have photos from all over the world, and in them my memories will last forever.

MOORE, MARLENE E.

I took the picture of the Blue Mosque from a cruise ship as it approached Istanbul, Turkey. Six graceful minarets adorn the mosque, one of Istanbul's most recognized landmarks. It was so beautiful! I took several photographs of the Blue Mosque and other mosques and museums. Design and construction of the Blue Mosque began in 1609 on the site of the old Imperial Palace. It is called the Blue Mosque because the interior is decorated with some 20,000 delicate blue tiles, 216 stained-glass windows, and geometric patterns complete the image. I am a retired dental hygienist living in Talladega, Alabama with my husband, John.

MORALES, JOSEPH M.

This was taken in the summer of 2007 at South Padre Island, Texas. I was with my son, Jesse, and godson, Ryan, enjoying the Gulf Coast. It is a series of pictures I took of the pelicans flying over us as we were on the beach. The sky was a grey scale—a very unusual sky. It looks as if a storm is approaching the island. I hope you enjoy "South Padre Island Sky."

MORRIS, MARCI LYNNE

This was taken at my favorite spot in Seattle. From Kerry Park, you can see the entire city and hear the sounds. Twilight is the coolest time of night, and best time to take pictures. I started this set of pictures at sunset, and this was the best shot. I love Seattle and love taking pictures all around the city.

MORTENSEN, CHERIE

I took several photos in the fall of 2007 which reflect the beauty of the state of Washington. This was taken in late October, shooting across Capitol Lake towards the state capitol. It was one of those days where you are grateful to be alive and I was enjoying the wonders of fall.

MURCHIE, TRISTEN R.

This photograph was taken at a random location on a freeway in Brisbane, Australia. It was 1:00 a.m. and I found myself wedged between two bridges and a cluster of pigeons while I captured the warming glow of artificial light streaking across a section of freeway, generally viewed from within a car at 100 kilometers per hour. This picture represents the potential that surrounds us. This seemingly void space transformed into a surreal, intriguing environment.

MURPHY, ALEXANDRA SIMONE

The day I took this picture, it started off with me feeling a great deal of emptiness and I had a billion things swarming around in my head. I ended up taking a walk through this pitch-black tunnel to clear my mind, and when I made my exit on the other side, I noticed several of these green objects on the ground. I found it to be a perfect opportunity to take a picture and ended up being pleased with the result. I'm not sure why I named it what I did, but that's the fun of it, I guess.

MYER, DONNA FOSTER

Sea turtles spend over ninety-five percent of their time far at sea, but breathe air. They can be badly injured struggling to escape from fishing nets and not escaping means death by drowning. Miss Lily, an immature female about fifteen years old, was hurt this way. By November 2007, she had healed. The South Carolina Aquarium released Miss Lily at the Isle of Palms. Standing hip-deep in surf, I caught her with these colorful reflections of the spectators wishing her "bon voyage!" That temporary transmitter, designed to safely fall off, documented her journey home for the education of her human friends.

NACAYTUNA, FATIMA ALVINEZ

"Winter At The Lake" is a photo of Mother Nature frozen in a cold winter morning. It preserves the evanescent beauty of water caught and trapped in the frigid environment, guarded by deciduous trees. Fatima A. Nacaytuna is a teacher who has worked with students from infancy to adulthood. Her experiences with people from all walks of life have enriched her perspectives that shaped her aesthetic view of the world. Her dynamic encounters have paved the way for the evolution of her artistry. Today, while she accomplishes her teaching tasks, she manages to stop and enjoy all forms of creative self-expression: poetry, photography, artwork, music, and meditation.

NASH, AARON RICHARD

This photo is of two students in my mom's class. My mom had a surprise birthday party given to her and these two girls tried on some of the objects my mom had to wear at her party. I took this picture because the girls look like they are having so much fun.

NEACE, SHELBY ERIN

A simple trip to the park is where my baby cousin, Carter, and I went. It was a beautiful day, with blue skies and light winds—perfect for picture taking. It just so happened that I had my camera with me and my friend, Kennedy, was there to take this priceless photo of the two of us. Staring at his little chubby cheeks and his cute bald head gave me a vibrant smile on my face. However, enjoying the time together with Carter and Kennedy was definitely the highlight of my day.

NELSON, BRENDA

This is a photograph of my granddaughter, Haylee. She loves to ham it up for anyone taking pictures and ofcourse, as her grandmother, I love taking pictures of her. Haylee is almost three in this picture. We thought she was just too cute in my old hat.

NELSON, KENNETH E.
I love the art of photography. I first started when I had a Kodak 126. When I was in high school I took a photography class. There I fell in love with black-and-white photographs. I always wanted to take better and more pictures. One day I hope to own my own darkroom.

NELSON, KRISTI JEAN
Jackalopes are real! This is a photograph of my daughter, Mikayla, wearing her Halloween costume that I made for her. Her dad recently moved to Wyoming, so she chose the jackalope in honor of him. After several days of sewing and inventing, we decided it was definitely worth some creative photos. I was really surprised at how well the costume turned out and we had a lot of fun taking these pictures. Kids are only young once, but I'll always have the pictures!

NEWMAN, MARY ALICE
This picture was taken in New York City, and I was very inspired by the crystal-clear reflections in the puddles all over the streets. There is a great juxtaposition between the dirty street puddle and the beautiful building, showing beauty can be found anywhere if you look for it.

NEWMAN, MICHAEL
Banjo, a name inspired by the instrument, both being high-strung and fast-paced, is my little terrier. She spends her days mostly sleeping, but when she's awake, she's full of energy and ready to play. Whether it's chasing squirrels out of the backyard, barking at the neighbor's cat through the fence, or her interminable fascination with the ball, she brings me much joy.

NICKHORN, ANDREAS
This photo is of a Michigan summer sunset. I felt so in awe of the incredible majesty of what had taken place before my eyes. It lasted only moments, but the sheer beauty has stayed with me much longer. I was so grateful to have snapped the shutter when I did.

NICOTRA, DAVID ALFIO
This photo was taken on my road trip. We stopped in Oregon to visit one of my friend's family members. While there, they took us around the country and I ran into a bunch of beautiful flowers. This one specifically caught my eye. God is so great for blessing us with such beauty.

NIEMAN, CRYSTAL LYNN
This photograph is of my precious daughter, Carilynn, who is forever amazed with what she finds in nature. Through her eyes, I'm able to find the natural beauty in the simple pleasures of life. It is amazing the way she can look at something and be so consumed with what it is. She is very curious and very smart for only being five. It is amazing what I can see when I look through the photo lens at my child—the pictures always capture the things you may not have noticed when you were there.

OCHOA, JANESSA
I'm a photography student at Miami International University of Art and Design studying photography. Photography is a great passion of mine, passed down through my family, yet I'm the first one who wants to do it as a career. This photo, "Window To The Skies," was taken on my way to Las Vegas. I had never been to the other side of the U.S. before, so I was really excited and I wanted to test out my new camera. Being up in the sky, you get a whole new perspective of the world with such beauty and wonder as shown in this picture. This will always be one of my favorites, and I'm honored to share it with everyone.

ODOM, RACHEL ELIZABETH
This is a photo I took during the summer of my tenth-grade year in 2007 when I went with my youth group from church to Tennessee for a fun week of whitewater rafting. This was by our campsite. I've always had the passion for photography, ever since I was a toddler. I always have my camera with me because I feel that there is always something to capture a picture of every day. I'm not known as Rachel, I'm known as, "Rachel and her camera," as my mom says I see everything through a camera lens.

OGUNBAMIYO, HOPE
This is a photo of my beautiful daughter, Ahrae. She and I were playing outside, and I was taking photos when she stuck her head out from behind the tree. I snapped the photo right away, and it came out perfect! If I had waited a second longer, the moment would have been lost. That is the thing I love most about being a photographer; you get to capture life's most memorable moments in time and freeze them for a lifetime. Capturing moments with children makes even better photos, because you get to keep them that way forever—long after they have grown and are no longer your precious baby. I read somewhere once, "Carry a camera, catch a memory," and I have had one with me every day since.

OSHIER, WILLIAM L.
In loving memory of one of the two Dachsunds who are my best friends in life. Peanut was fifteen-and-a-half years old at the time of this picture. I was forced to put her down right before Christmas 2007 due to health problems. Peanut was a true friend. Her unconditional love helped carry me through the ups and downs of life's journey. We will always love and miss her. God's blessings come in many ways, and Peanut was one of them. I will be ever grateful for the time we were able to spend together.

OSWALD, FAHRINISA FATIMA KEVSER
This photo was taken during low tide on the bay side of Eastham, Cape Cod, where my family owns a vacation house. I took "Cape Cod, Low Tide" with my Canon 30D digital SLR camera. I am an aspiring photojournalist, but enjoy doing photography of all sorts, including portraiture and landscape photography, the category in which this photo falls. One thing that always makes a photograph memorable for me is the perspective from which it was taken; therefore, when I am doing my own photography, I always try to find that unique perspective.

OWEN, MAX L.
Living in Anchorage, Alaska we often enjoy moose and other wildlife up close. The mother was nearby, but I only got a picture of the twins trying to decide who got to be in the pool. Later that night, the twins and mom were in the yard again. The twins were playing with the grandchildren's beach ball. They didn't pop it.

OWENS, KIMBERLY A.
I have a passion for taking photos of my children. There are so many moments where they come alive with beauty and energy. This is a photo of my six-year-old daughter, Olivia Leigh. She truly glows in a way that takes my breath and melts my heart. She tends to have the same effect on everyone she meets. Her sweet, chatty personality affirms the angel in her. Olivia is a twin to Hudson and has a baby brother, Hayden, who is three. They provide giggles that make photo opportunities magical. They all bring indescribable joy to our lives.

PADILLA, CHANTELLE RAE
My fiancé, Frank Anthony, and I had our son, Frank Colin Fregoso, in August of 2007. Since then, our favorite time of the day is bathtime. As Frankie undresses little Frank, he starts to giggle and play—he knows it's bathtime! I love capturing his many smiles so I can share them with family and friends.

PAGE, BRIAN KENT
We got Payton in November 1999. By coincidence, our neighbor had also gotten a Beagle puppy at the same time named Ty. Ty would come over to play with Payton and they became the best of friends. After talking with the neighbor, we came to the conclusion that both puppies were from the same litter. So not only were they best friends, they were also true brothers. After some abuse and neglect, Ty came to live with us permanently in the summer of 2000. Reunited, they will never be separated again.

PARATCHEK, ARIANNA RENEE
Photography is my favorite pastime—I never go anywhere without my camera. I'm always taking pictures, especially when there are animals around. These horses belong to my stepfather. Chy and Trigger, the two in front, are best friends. The one in the back is Easy, she's our newest horse. The two boys don't like her much, so this represents them wonderfully. I think it shows their personalities as well, Chy is laid back, Trigger is crazy and playful, and Easy is an attention seeker. These horses are my best friends, and now I can have them, personalities and all, right in my living room.

PARTON, ELIZABETH ANN
This is my son, Tristan, poised on a fence in a nearby park. Others always ask, "Why didn't he smile?" But a picture is not always about smiling. It is a real-life moment captured forever. Tell me, can you imagine what he is dreaming of?

PASIC, RAMIZ
This photo was taken on my way to dinner with some friends I met in a hostel. It was a wet night and I just liked how the street was lit up with peo-

ple, even though it was raining. It was a spur-of-the-moment shot standing under my "brolly," and I just tried to capture the moment.

PATTERSON, KEVIN S.
On a chilly November morning this bald eagle took a break from hunting to dry off during an ice fog in southwest Alaska. The photographer, Kevin Patterson, is most know for his very unique and custom creations of automotive photographic art for his clients. However, a passion of his is wildlife and the conservation of it for generations to come. He has several websites and we hope you enjoy more of his work. Kevin loves to share his knowledge and help others enjoy photography.

PATTERSON, SHERRY
This photo was taken in my backyard in Georgia. I used to sit and watch over baby chicks while they scratched feed. I got up and when I walked away and turned back, I saw this chicken sitting on the gun. It was a pet which followed me everywhere. It was waiting for me to return. I ran and got my camera and snapped this picture—a rare moment, in my opinion.

PEASE, RITA ANTOINETTE
Harry and Kim, this is in appreciation for all you do for Dad and me. Your high altitude location and home is so beautiful. My friend and I were walking in Central Park when this bird came flying down and rested in a nearby bush. I managed to get a few good shots of this beautiful bird, but this one was by far the best. I am a working student and I enjoy various forms of artistic expression. I love being around wildlife more than most other things. I want to thank my good friend, Becca, for bringing me into the park; otherwise, this awesome photograph would have never become a reality.

PEEBLES, JACQUELINE ANNE
This is a photograph of my daughter, Jayme, and one of our Husky pups. I love the innocent love between dogs and humans—it just glows and I wanted to catch that emotion and keep it alive forever. I am an animal lover. Jayme is my oldest daughter and she takes a stunning picture. The Husky's name is Crystal and I have named this photograph "Baby Doll."

PETERSON, RACHEL ANN
The seventy-two-year age difference between Brooklyne and her grandfather seemed all but nonexistent this particular spring day. Although she had been camping before, Brooklyne had never had the opportunity to go fishing. She had a blast learning how to fish and Grandpa was never so patient in teaching her. Putting the rod together, baiting the hook, and casting the line, she tried so hard to contain her excitement while they waited for a fish to bite. Imagine Brooklyne's reaction when she felt a small tug. Bursting at the seams, she proudly showed off her first catch to the family.

PHELAN, CHRISTOPHER
I took this photo two years ago on a family vacation in Hawaii. This hibiscus was on the island of Kona. I like this photo because of how the bright pink part of the flower is constrasted with the white petals. The use of my wide-angle lens also turned out well. In a few months I will be graduating from Arizona State University. Photography has been a hobby of mine since high school and I plan to keep pursuing it.

PHELPS, HEATHER
I am a stay-at-home mom with a great ambition to be a photographer. I love photography and capturing the moments in that time. This photo was taken of my son at a park across the street from my grandmother's house in October of 2007. He was in very deep thought and concentration watching his older sister and my grandmother with her dog. He was very curious as to what they were doing, and you can see that in the picture. I love that about this picture, and it is what I try to capture in about every picture I take—still moments in time!

PIANTADOSI, DEBBIE
This is my first grandchild in Cancun. It shows the joy that a grandchild can bring into your life. Since Seth was born, we have a new granddaughter, Alyssa, and another boy on his way. This photo shows the pure innocence of a child.

PICKELSIMER, BELINDA LEE
This is a photo of my daughter, Caraline, and her older cousin, Elyssa. I cherish this photo because it reflects the love that these beautiful little girls share for each other and the world around them. I love to take pictures, especially of my family. Photos are the secrets of our world—a link to the past, present, and future.

PIEDRAHITA, CATALINA
This photograph is a piece of a body of work called "Paint And Skin." It's a series I combined using traditional black-and-white photography and painting, using the human body as a canvas and the camera to preserve the ephemeral beauty of body art. My purpose was to create an environment where photography and painting would come together producing an artwork in which media and genres would blur all for the sake of art, craft, and beauty.

PIERRE, JASON
I've always had slight interest in film and photography, but did not focus on it much, until one day I just felt like taking pictures for no reason at all. Of course, I took pictures of moving objects and items for ebay, but my favorite type of picture is the candid shot. I focused on my subject when she was not looking, catching a beautiful gaze that she could never do on purpose. Looking at her closer, it seems more perfect than it was at the time. It truly exemplifies the harmless pleasure of dreaming and aspiration. I am currently a graduating senior at Bowling Green State University. I'll be getting a bachelor's and am wondering what my next big move will be. I love to travel, draw, watch movies, and solve puzzles and anticipate starting successful companies in the future involving clothing, show production, and music.

POPOVA, NATALIA
This is an image of the ice lagoon in Iceland—it is a whole different world out there. As the reflection of the ice in the lake reflected on the mirror in my camera, I felt the icy purity of nature. It was a beautiful sight to behold.

POPOW, LORRIE
This amusing photograph is of my grandsons in their safari outfits. Meet my grandsons, Joseph, Cameron, Jace, and Phoenix. As they say, "The uniform makes the man," and as soon as these young men put their outfits on, they were ready to serve. All were very serious until we looked down at their shoes. It's funny now, but in time we know they will fill even bigger shoes, and then the joke will be on us. I'm an egg artist, and can be found decorating eggshells on most days. However, during vacation time, you'll find me having fun with my grandsons.

PRADO, MARGARETH LYRA
This is a photo of my niece, Louiza, holding her dreams of her fairytales in our backyard—imagining she is a blue water fairy.

PRANSKEVICH, JESSICA MARIE
The picture was taken on the way into Chicago. I think it gives a glimpse of nature's beauty in its most pure form—untouched by Man and made by Mother Nature.

PRINGLE, CHARLOTTE N.
I took this beautiful photograph while sailing the waterways of Russia. I stuck my head out of my stateroom window to get a picture of the sunset and got the added bonus of a bird in mid-flight. I've never been the best photographer so I was especially pleased with the beauty of this shot.

PROPPS, ARTHUR GENE, JR.
This photograph is of my two dogs. Anesthesia is a year-old Shar Pei and Floyd is an eight-year-old Husky-Shar Pei mix.

RAINS, LORI S.
This photograph is of Arlington National Cemetery in October. A dear friend, Lt. Col. Joel Craddock, took my sisters and I on a tour there. The scenery was breathtaking. It was a picture-perfect moment of silence.

RANSOME, MEGAN
This is a photograph of my cat, Tiger Lily, with a water droplet on her nose. She frequently has a water droplet on her nose after drinking out of the fish tank. I thought it would be beautiful to capture both her and the water droplet. I love to capture the beauty of animals and nature in my photos. I am from a town called Aurora in Ontario, Canada and will be turning twenty-two this year. I plan on keeping my hobby of photography alive as long as I live, no matter how little time I have.

RAUGHT, CHAD MICHAEL
Chad Raught lives with his wife, Susan, and five children in Phoenix, Arizona. This photograph of their youngest child, Raeann, was taken in the family's backyard. It was her first Easter. There was a moment where Raeann looked like she was praying, so we snapped the photograph. It will be a keepsake for many years to come.

READ, CARISSA NICOLE

My name is Carissa Read. I am sixteen years old and I currently live in a small town in Mississippi. This picture was taken on my first mission trip to Reynosa, Mexico. Although the majority of the Reynosa children responded well to our outreach that day, this child did not. However, he stayed glued to his window and watched. As I observed his stubborn resistance, childlike desire, and meek surroundings, I had a small peek into his life. Though this picture cannot truly capture my experience, I hope it will help you appreciate what you have as it did me.

REILLY, WILLIAM J. G.

This photograph was taken out front of my grandparents' cottage. I got very lucky with the water drip from the oar creating a ripple effect toward the canoe. It was extremely difficult to take this photograph, as I was in the canoe holding the oar with my left hand and the camera with my right hand while leaning out of the canoe. Unfortunately, the camera I used to take this photograph was destroyed a few weeks later as I attempted to take an up-close shot of a rapid river fall when I lost my balance and fell into the water.

REW, KEARSTIN

This is a photo of the St. Marks Lighthouse. I laugh every time I see this picture because it reminds me about how I was standing thigh-deep in the water, but I absolutely love the fact that the pelican was captured soaring so freely.

RINK, KASI G.

I'm a soldier in the United States Army stationed at Fort Lewis, Washington. As I was exploring the state, I came upon this sunset on the beach, I found it breathtaking and mesmerizing. It was a sight I felt I should share with the world. I wish society was as peaceful as the sunset.

RITCHIE, TABITHA JAYNE

This is a photo of an early morning walk on the beach. I am always looking for the next photo opportunity, and when I saw this sunrise, I knew it would be a keepsake, I love photography, art, and truly hope that this picture reminds you of your favorite "sunrise at the beach!"

ROBBS, NICHOLAS FLOYD

I live in the country in southeastern Arizona. My family owns and operates Robbs Farm, which my grandfather started over fifty years ago. While living out here, I've grown to appreciate scenes of rural life—bull riding, a country sunset, and branding a four-wheeler stunt that probably should not have been attempted.

ROBILLARD, KYLE M.

This is a photo of my friend, Dylan, from a skate trip we took to New York City. I love to shoot skateboarding because it gives me an opportunity to hang out with great friends, travel, and capture moments like this one.

ROBINSON, JONATHAN ROBERT

As a striving amateur photographer, I am always looking for different shots at different locations. I was in New York City, New York when I discovered this amazing angle. It was so intimidating

that I knew I had to capture it on film. I want to take this time to thank Picture.com and the International Library of Photography for this opportunity. Without photography in the world, there would be a lot more closed eyes in society. Life moves too fast, but I can freeze time when I am behind the camera.

ROBINSON, RUSSELL ELLISE

My name is Russell Robinson and this is a photo of my nephew, Coen Robinson. We were at the Portland Zoo almost all day and my nephew was getting hungry, so my brother, Roger, my sister-in-law, Peggy, my niece, Summer, and I went to McDonald's to eat and that is when I could not resist taking a picture of my nephew because he was enjoying himself, eating his french fries.

RODRIGUEZ, MELVIN

My wife and I were strolling along the beach during low tide. I decided to walk ahead so I could write something romantically "sappy" in the sand for her. As I covered some distance, I turned to glance at her and realized the opportunity to hold her in my hands at this distance. I chose this specific title because I would take her everywhere with me. Even after ten years of marriage, I still miss her when I go to work for the day.

ROMERO, JASON RONALD

This is a photograph of my dog, Luecious, this photo was taken on a November, San Diego afternoon at Kate Sessions Park on Pacific Beach, California. I used a Canon AE-1 Program, 50mm lens with 400-speed film. I love to take photographs of everything I feel is an inspiration at the moment. I try to act fast, for this is the moment I want to capture and keep forever and always. I am currently going to school for photography. I am taking classes here and their to help me learn different techniques—there is always something new to learn. I don't care who you are, there is always something fun and exciting to learn in the field of photography.

RUBY, ROBIN CAROL

As an amateur photographer, I captured this photo of a boy running on the beach using, for the first time, the stop-action feature on my Nikon D50. Since then I've taken several hundred photos using the feature and have been delighted with nearly all of them.

RUVALCABA, DANIEL

Clarissa is our tiny miracle. She can't walk, talk, roll over or sit up without assistance. She can, however, show love. This picture shows a miracle in progress. There are many faces to our angel most wouldn't understand, but when we sat her in this chair next to this squishy duck, she looked down at it and you could "hear" the expression on her face, "You came from where?" I suppose we should be grateful that she doesn't fully understand. Nonetheless, we'll take one tiny miracle at a time.

RYAN, THERESA

As a young girl, I always had a passion for taking pictures, but never had the time because of work and family. Now getting up in years and being a survivor of cancer four times, I have more time on

my hands and a greater appreciation for God's creations. He gave me life when I thought there was none. He gave me hope. I owe Him my every breath. I thank God for the opportunity to share His beauty with the world.

SALGADO, ELSY ALICIA

"Felicidad En Pobreza" was taken in Tiquisate, Guatemala. It is a photograph of my sister and our three cousins. This was the first time my cousins had ever seen a camera, and their faces lit up and their smiles grew from cheek to cheek. I took this picture because the look of happiness, despite their unfortunate surroundings, is something beautiful to cherish and a very humbling experience to learn from.

SAMUEL, MECHELLE M.

This is a photo of my grandkids, seven-year-old Danyla and four-year-old Darrow Goins III. We were doing a promotion for the Christmas holiday. I'm always amazed at what kind of expression they are going to give me. When I have the camera in my hand, they are always ready to pose for a picture. My main focus after retirement will be photo work and to also have a studio.

SANCHEZ, LUPE A.

This is a photograph of my puppy, Adora. She is seventeen months in this Christmas picture. My daughter, Valerie, got the puppy when she was two months old, but she had to move and she could'nt take her with her, so I adopted Adora and she has been with me ever since. She was a good girl to pose for this picture, "Santa's Helper." I love her so much—she is a good dog. and she is part of the family.

SANSOM, JULIE

Dingoes are a huge part of my life. I keep pure-bred dingoes as part of Victoria's Captive Breeding Program. Pure-bred dingoes are endangered due to interbreeding with domestic dogs, etc. They make fantastic companions and they keep me entertained and always on my toes. Bruce and Az are very photogenic and I always have a camera handy. This photo shows their true spirit and character.

SANTIAGO, IRIS E.

Lucky loves to sit in front of open windows during sunny days. This particular day, the blinds were slightly opened and the shadow over his body was amazing.

SCHAEFER, ANNE

I snapped this picture while touring Angkor Wat in Cambodia in 2006. This picture symbolizes God's warm, loving arms wrapping themselves around Man's heart of stone, and His love seeding and taking root.

SCHALL, MANDA CELESTE

This photo is of my best friend, Caity Stonaker, while we were at Bar Harbor, Maine during the summer of 2006. I'm seventeen years old and I attend high school at Northampton. I plan to go to school for photography and become a photographer. This was the first contest I entered, and I'm thrilled to know my snapshot is published. It's an amazing feeling of accomplishment.

SCHELL, JENNA LAYNE

This is a photo of children that I took during a stop at a Hmong village along the Mekong Delta in Laos. The children were curiously observing other visitors, and I managed to capture the shot as I lagged behind. The photo was taken during a six-month travel stint to Southeast Asia and Australia. Since the trip, I've gone back to school, and am currently studying graphic design, which includes some photography. This has provided me with the opportunity to produce some more amazing photos to add to the many from my travels. After completion of my schooling, I hope to travel more, and to take many beautiful pictures.

SCHUBERT, CINDY LEA

I love to photograph my pets—they are always doing something to make me laugh. I have two cats and two dogs and there is something funny going on all the time. This is my Manx, China, watching Animal Planet, his favorite channel. He will watch the dog shows for hours.

SCHWARTZ, AARON

This photo is one of several photos that I took over the Atlantic Ocean. I love being able to look at our world from a different perspective. There was a great cloud cover that day. I felt like I could step out and walk across the sky.

SCIONE, MARK ROBERT, JR.

My name is Mark, but everyone knows me as "Scone." I have been interested in art since as far back as I can remember. I have been selling my art for about seven years now. Aside from photography, I also enjoy drawing, painting, sculpture, tattoo design, illustration, and game design, among other things. I also write short stories, song lyrics, and I like to party.

SCOTT, CARRIE ANN

I was on my first trip to Italy and my friend had requested some specific shots while I was there. She wanted a photo of some old guys just "shootin' the breeze," chatting, and hanging out as they do. I found these fabulous men in Vernazza. It turned out to be one of my favorites for sure! I'm currently organizing a new photo site, but in the meantime, I'm the creative director and owner of a graphic design firm in Abbotsford, British Columbia, Canada.

SELF, LAURIE GAYLE

I had rousted my roommate out of bed at 4:30 on a Sunday to see if I could get some good landscapes of mist on the water at my favorite park. As I was packing up my tripod, I noticed a tree floating by. When it got closer, I realized it was one of our very reclusive beavers making repairs to the lodge. I was lucky enough to catch him on the way by, because just after I snapped this, he dove effortlessly under water, taking that whole huge branch with him. Thank you to my friend, Ria, for helping me name the photo.

SERAK, PAT A.

This is the view from my kitchen window, after a snowfall in December. I remember joyfully thanking God for the good gift of the beautiful snow. As the Bible says, "Every good gift and every perfect gift is from above." The way this photo turned out was another good gift. It captured the peace of God and peace with God that I had through the Lord Jesus Christ when I took it.

SEYMOUR, BONNIE LU

I took this picture on a camping trip. My son, T. J., is facing the camera. My son-in-law, Anthony, has his back to the camera. I was trying to get a nice picture of my son without him knowing I was taking it, and this is what I got. He was 18 years old and getting ready to leave for the army.

SHEA, JEFFREY JOHN

This photo was taken in Badlands National Park in November of 2007. While on a cross-country trip to my new home of Phoenix, Arizona I experienced seeing a live badger for the first time. This photo was shot from my vehicle—it was a difficult shot to take because he kept crawling in and out of his burrow, but I finally got the perfect shot. This photo is one of many wildlife photos taken on that trip, but this one I was particularly proud of.

SHELLHORN, LINA CAMPOS

I'm not a professional photographer, but my hobby is taking pictures for souvenirs. I'm a Filipina married to my husband, Kleve, and currently residing in Thatcher, Arizona. We're on our way to Las Vegas for our second-year wedding anniversary when these beautiful mountains and river caught my attention; I asked my hubby to stop. The outcome was very nice.

SHELLNUT, AMANDA ELSIE

I've had the pleasure of attending Northern Michigan University, where I've received my bachelor's of fine arts in photography with a minor in Native American studies. My studies and my family brought me to where I am today. It's great when I can share my work and have those I love be a part of it. My image is of my new sister, Amy, and her daughter, Mackenzie, on their big day.

SHULL, MICHAEL TODD

I enjoy taking pictures and I am always looking for the perfect snapshot. This just happened to be one of those moments that was captured perfectly.

SILAS, JESSICA

This picture was taken just before sunrise on a lake in Wisconsin. It was painful waking up early in the morning, but I'm thrilled I did. The sun had not yet had a chance to burn off the fog covering the lake, so it created a perfect, serene image as it enveloped the rustic dock. I love being able to capture precious moments with only a click, and therefore I always have a camera at my side. I'm a student at the University of Illinois, Urbana-Champaign, studying environmental science and hope to continue photography as a hobby.

SILBEREISEN, KANE MATTHEW

This photograph was taken on the jungle train from Gemas to Kota Bharu in Malaysia. It was my first time abroad with my brother, Aaron. I had my camera ready at all times. I feel the composition is what makes this photograph so striking. The subject, a Gemas local, was completely unaware of me vertically standing above him. "Jungle Train" is clearly my favorite photograph of the thousands I took.

SIMMERING, ANDREW LEROY

I love to paint and often photograph subjects I might want to try my hand at, but when I took a vacation with my wife and son to Moab, Utah, I saw colors and shapes in nature that could take a lifetime to capture. The afternoon that "Monumental" was taken, we had driven all day from our home in Loveland, Colorado. We took the back way along the Colorado River into Moab. This took us right through Monument Valley where so many of the great Western films had been done. This photo was the first of hundreds that I took over the next week throughout Arches National Park and Canyonlands National Park. I am not a professional photographer, but I do have an eye for what will make a good photograph. Everyone must see this place, it will change you forever!

SMITH, DOUGLAS L.

I took this photo the first time I saw the sun after a huge snowstorm. When I looked outside that morning, I rushed to get my camera. My photography has always centered on the outdoors, primarily focusing on quality rather than quantity.

SMITH, MAXINE MASTERFIELD

I am a fine artist on Siesta Key, Florida. Every year a pair of yellow-crowned night herons came to a pine tree nearby. They built their nest and laid eggs. When the babies hatched, I climbed up on the roof to photograph them. After becoming teenagers, they flew away. The saddest part of this story is that the neighbors who owned the 100-year-old tree tore it down to build a swimming pool. Where do the herons go now? When I look out of my studio window today, I see a tall, faded umbrella, where the tree once stood.

SMITH, SUE

In 2004 I retired as a dispatcher from the Anaheim Police Department. I moved to the rural community of Michie, Tennessee. For years I have tried to keep my camera near in case I happened upon that "Kodak moment." My photo was taken in November 2007 when I went to visit my daughter, Angela Welch, in Fayetteville, Arkansas. As I was nearing her home on Drewry's Bluff, the skies lit up with sunrays spreading out in all directions. I prayed that it would last until I arrived and could get a picture. It's hard to be God's natural beauty!

SOMERS, PAUL A.

This photo was taken from my home in Colorado spring in early December 2007. The mountain is Pikes Peak, which dominates our view west from any point in Colorado Springs.

SOO-MAWSTON, WENDY

"The Aubergine Family" is from the series "Time-Consuming Consequences." It looks at everyday food presented in an alternative way, with the influence of personal experiences. This photograph addresses the ideal family: two parents, children, a house and garage, and a plot of land, all protected by a fence, an ideal that may no longer exist in current times. It was created in a studio and captured on a large format camera.

SOPCZAK, NICHOLAS ADAM

Some close friends of mine and I were climbing a classic multi-pitch route as the Cheakamus River roared beneath us, making for a truly blissful experience. After taking a moment to soak it all in I was fortunate to capture this great moment. The west coast of British Columbia is a photographer's delight, full of urban events, nature, and adventure. While setting up my new life on the coast, Raw Spectra Photography was born. I am excited and eagerly anticipate great things for myself and Raw Spectra. "The time with the most change is the time for most possibility."

SPENCER, NATALIE ANNE

I really love the zoo, and I love all types of monkeys. It's such a challenge taking pictures of crazy animals, and I think that's why I like it so much. When I saw these monkeys in the back of their cage cleaning each other, I knew it would be the perfect picture. I had over 100 pictures at the end of the day, but this one was my favorite. What's better than catching wild animals being quite civilized?

SPRADLING, CARLA LEANN

This photo was taken my freshman year in high-school at the Dallas Arboretum on a field trip. It has since been one of my favorites. I would like to thank the people who have helped me most in life, my parents, Don and Diane, my sisters, Christy and Carrie, my best friend, Jordan Zimmerman, and my high school English teacher, Mrs. Linda Muhl—without your love and support my goals could never be attained.

STEELE, SAMUEL LIN

I caught these boys on the train from Kanchanaburi to Bangkok. We were just getting off the train, so I only saw them for a few seconds. The last three years, I've been touring with a Disney on Ice show, which has taken me around the world and back. At twenty-two, I feel so blessed to have been able to build a portfolio full of photos just as magical as "A Thai Welcome."

STEINMETZ, CELSIE I.

They say a picture is worth a thousand words. When I took this photo, the things that stood out to me were the vivid colors, the small details in the wood grain, and how perfectly everything fit together, almost like a puzzle. This photo tells its own story without saying a word. I have found that being in the right place at the right time has a lot to do with capturing beautiful photographs. Hopefully this will be the first of many beautiful images I will be publishing in my future career.

STEINMETZ, KELSEY MARIE

This beautiful picture of my cat, Cali, was taken a week after I got her from a close friend of mine. I wanted to take some pictures of her and her sister, Pumpkin, who was playing by a fence at the time. I brought them outside from the barn and they began playing the moment I put them down. I just happened to capture this amazing photo of her focusing on a flower.

STETTER, JOANNE

This photo was among the first taken with my new camera and definitely is a favorite. "Hunting Honey" was taken with an 8.0 Olympus Stylus 800. The camera was given to me as a gift for Christmas 2006. I was anxious to try out the camera, so I stepped out my front door to find some bees buzzing in my azalea bushes. My intention was to take a photograph of the azaleas in bloom, but was pleasantly surprised by this little fellow hunting honey.

STEWARD, CHRISTOPHER MORGAN

This is a photograph of a sunset I took after a day at the beach in South Haven, Michigan. I have often heard people say that pictures last a lifetime, and that phrase holds very true. This photograph is definitely an image of a lifetime that I will never forget.

STEWART, DENISE ANN

This picture was taken at my mother's home on the Georgian Bay. It depicts the awesome beauty of the North and makes you realize how amazing Mother Nature really is.

STEWART, JENNIFER

This is a photo of my daughter and her dog. I thought that it was a good picture. My daughter, who is three years old at this time, grew up with this dog—she taught her how to climb the fence. She loves this dog. Her dog's name is Demon. I take a lot of photos of my kids.

STEWART, KATIE ELIZABETH

This is the sixth photograph in a series of ten. This is a demonstration of time traveling through different moments in a counter-clockwise direction. The concept questions the importance of time in nature. There are no lifeforms present because their absence illuminates the meaning of time if we are unaware of it passing.

STEWART, KRISTEN R.

This is a picture of my beautiful two-year-old, Piper. She loves to pretend she's driving. On this particular day, I believe she was driving her sister, Ziva, and I to Wal-Mart. I snapped the picture and just loved the look on her face. I couldn't resist sending it in.

STIDMAN, ALICE MARIE

This was taken during the time when my grandparents departed for a road trip, leaving us in charge of the ranch. One day we went to feed the animals. Madison Katelyn Stidman could not take her eyes off of the flowers that were in bloom. The garden was not completely in bloom until Madison crawled inside. With my camera at hand, I was able to capture "Grandma's Garden In Full Bloom." This was a wonderful year for me because I just finished my bachelor's degree and my husband and I celebrated our third anniversary with anticipation for our baby's arrival. I love to capture life's finest moments.

STOLWORTHY, LLOYD

My Uncle Joe inspired this photo when he played with Chet. For the last fifteen years he went to Nashville for two weeks in July for the CAAS Convention. CAAS stands for Chet Atkins Appreciation Society. Chet passed away on June 30, ten days before they were to meet. I received pictures of Joe playing this guitar and I took pictures of it in Las Vegas, Nevada fourteen days later at a convention, knowing Chet was the highlight of Joe's life. I owe it all to Joseph Cisco Haynes II, better known as J. C. to his friends and family. Thanks for reading my story. I was lucky to have been in the right place and time.

STONE, RACHAEL NICOLE

I graduated from high school in May 2007 and I would be attending college in the fall. I wanted to make my summer one that I would remember forever. After some fundraising, I went with my church youth group on a mission trip to El Salvador. As I was walking through one of the villages, I looked over to the side of the street and saw this beautiful little girl. I was struck with sadness by the conditions she was living in. It set into motion the goals I have chosen to set for myself. This trip changed my life.

STOUT, MARTHA M.

I have always enjoyed photography, even as a little girl. My favorite photographs are taken with a macro lens so that I can shoot up close to flowers and insects. I also like taking pictures of landscapes and sunsets. I will always treasure photographs taken by loved ones.

STREITBERGER, MARCIA KAY

This photo was taken at our good friends, Bob and Judy's house in Palm Springs, California. We watched this mother hatch her young and then feed them until were ready to leave the nest. I have always loved taking pictures, especially of our kids, Mike, Justin, and Stephanie, and my husband, Bill. Now that the kids are grown and on their own, I've turned to nature. That is, until grandchildren come along one day.

STUDLEY, LAUREN K.

While visiting a shrine in Nagoya, Japan, I was delighted and impressed with the Japanese aesthetic. While photographing a small baptism service at the shrine, I couldn't help but stray to the beautiful shrine maidens. Their hair was pefect and their clothes crisp and clean. This was a vision of another world that my friends and family back in Idaho could only dream of.

SUKERT, MICHELLE

While living in Miami, Florida I have noticed not only the unique cultures of this city, but the beauty behind nature. "A Diamond In The Rough" was taken at Fairchild Tropical Gardens in Coconut Grove, Florida, which is a home to many different flowers and plants. This flower stuck out to me the most because of the smoothness and contrast of colors. This picture gives off the feeling that even the smallest light will shine through the dark.

SULLIVAN, CONRAD CHARLES JOHN

This is a photo of my pet dog, Jackson. I took this picture of him on the first snow of the '07-'08 winter season. Jackson is a vibrant, young dog that will keep you going. He is also the sweetest and most gentle dog there is. He loves to chase lacrosse balls and bees, and play Frisbee.

SULLIVAN, STEPHANIE ANNE

I titled this photo "Honesty" because when looking at it, I can see so much in the subject's expression. One can always know the truth when looking someone in the eyes.

SULTEMEIER, LESLIE LYNN
This picture is unique, because I live in Texas and we don't see ice, let alone waterfalls freezing up. The ice and the people that day were so beautiful and colorful! I couldn't pass up a beautiful moment and day. I just thought, "Wow, how lucky am I to see this." I was so shocked because I never thought I would see such a beautiful place! I can't believe I caught a moment such as that. I cant wait to see how different next year will be!

SWARTS, JOHN P.
This picture was taken while camping at Pennsylvania's beautiful Lackawanna State Park in October 2006. I had risen before dawn and brought my camera down to the lake. I spooked a few turkeys as I approached in the unseasonably cold air. To my great delight, I noticed one had walked straight across the dock and left its prints in the frost. I took multiple shots of this once-in-a-lifetime event and I am very pleased with this photo in particular. This photo reminds me of the beautiful sights I experienced that weekend and how bitterly cold I was while sleeping in my tent!

SWIEBODA, MACIEJ
This photo was taken hours after birth. A baby girl and her mother are captured at the moment where no other people exist for both of them. There is nothing more beautiful than a pure, true innocent love.

SZYMANSKI, DONALD
This photograph of Yosemite Falls was taken during my visit with a van tour from San Francisco. It has been years since I had gone to Yosemite Falls for a visit. I have lived in Laurence Harbor for fifty-nine-and-a-half years. I have my DVD movie collection—well over 450 movies. I have my cat, as she keeps us both company. I have a very special vacation trip planned for April 2008, for my sixtieth birthday.

TABARACCI, VICTORIA
Every day people face stuggles, and every day people give up. This picture represents taking things head on, without fear or regret. No matter how big and bad the monster may be, you have to fight in order to win. There are no exceptions.

TAKAMAA, MIKAEL MATIAS
This photo was taken during our vacation to Newfoundland this summer. This is our friend, Ian, fishing at Dancing Point on the Humber River near Cornerbrook. This photo was taken with my Sony Alpha and has not been altered in any way. Sunsets in Newfoundland can be dramatic as the sun slips over the horizon and the reflections off the water are quite beautiful. I am just starting to learn photography, and it's something I really enjoy. I'm a retired military member who is studying to be a graphic artist.

TANGEL, KRISTIN CLAIRE
I enjoy photographing birds, as well as action shots, and this was no exception. The best way to caption this photo is a line from "The Sound of Music" song, "My Favorite Things": "Wild geese that fly with the moon on their wings."

TAYLOR, CARLA MAE
I took this photo of my daughter and her horse for our 4-H group. We love our horses very much. My kids have been around horses all of their lives. Our horses are our family. We live on a farm in Ridgefield, Washington. We have six other horses. My two daughters and I ride and train our own horses. I was very pleased when I saw how special this photo was. It touched my heart.

TAYLOR, SARAH DOLLY MINNIE
I have always enjoyed photography and my niece, Abigial, always enjoys getting her picture taken. So I am constantly taking pictures of her—this picture is one of my favorites. I love how Abigail's blue eyes pop in the picture and how elegant she looks!

TENNISCO, HILDA BERNADINE
I thought my life couldn't be more complete, then, my first grandchild arrived. Precious Emma arrived on January 23, 2002. I didn't realize how much more a person could be blessed. Grandchildren are so very special. When I look at precious Emma, I am blessed with reflections of when my children were small. I see so much of Emma's dad, my firstborn son, in her. Emma gives me so much. When I see my children in her, I'm able to relive those special times of caring for my own children. I've been blessed even more with three more grandchildren. Though they are all loved and treated the same, the first always holds a special place. That first grandchild paves the way for the rest and makes your journey so much easier. I love you, precious Emma and thank you for being you, my granddaughter.

TERRY, MISTY DAWN
This is a photo of my garden, which is always covered with butterflies. I took this picture with a simple digital camera that I got for Christmas from my husband last year. We are currently living in Pulaski, Tennessee. We moved here to be with family while my husband is deployed to Iraq for the fourth time, and is serving fifteen months. So I take pride in this photo, since he was the one who gave the camera to me. It was just a random picture I took that came out very well. I enjoy my gardens very much and hope I can take many more that show the beauty of nature!

THILL, RODNEY HOWARD
This is a photo that I took while I was on top of a volcano in Maui. The view from up that high was spectacular, so I started taking pictures. As I was looking through the pictures later on, I noticed this one and I was amazed. I then found out that photography could be one of my many talents. I also enjoy cooking, singing, and acting.

THOMPSON, RACHEL ZE
In Australia there is a children's song titled, "Never Smile at a Crocodile." I thought this an apt title as the crocodile looks like he/she is smiling. This photo was taken of a saltwater crocodile in captivity in Darwin, Australia. At the time of taking the photo, I was encouraging my partner to appetize the crocodile with his finger through the fence to enable me to get a better picture. He was somewhat uncooperative at the time; however, I still managed to capture the intricate details of the crocodile's facial expression through his/her eye.

TIPTON, RACHEL
I took this picture nearly a year ago. It is the last photograph I took of my cat, Sampson—sadly, he died about a week later. I am truly thankful for having a great cat to model for me. He always seemed to like the camera. He loved milk and it seemed like he could smell it from a mile away. He was quite the entertainer and he will remain in our memories forever.

TOBOROWSKY, LINDA
Taken by photographer, writer, talkshow host, Linda Toborrowsky, this photograph of William captures his usual statuesque pose in the family room. From humble beginnings in the midst of a commercial construction site by the ocean on Amelia Island, William has lovingly journeyed north to a peaceful, swank, and simple life atop the West Virginia mountains. This photo expresses William's demeanor as he spends time with family and friends watching television and before one of his many catnaps. The deep, rich colors surrounding him, coupled with his elegant stature, emit the royalty of his prestigious poise and majestic name.

TOWE, ROBIN L.
This is a picture of a little girl that I ran across in public. I am always taking pictures and enjoy candid black-and-white pictures the best. This is the first contest I have entered and am excited that my photo was chosen. I live in Missouri with my husband and daughter, and enjoy taking pictures. I have been taking pictures most of my life. I am working on doing more with my photography.

TREASTER, MARTIN JOHN ROBERT
This is a picture of one of my classmates. It was taken in my home, as well as approximately 100 other pictures of her. I have done quite a few other photo shoots, but this is the first time I've entered any of my pictures in a contest. I was pleasantly surprised to find out that my photo was entered into the semifinals. I am finishing my education for visual communications, and I am working toward starting my own studio.

TREMBLAY, DANIELLE
Danielle has been an avid photographer since getting her own digital camera. Her photographs include many different subjects including numerous self-portraits.

TUMIEL-KOZAK, EVA R.
I got my first camera as a child from my father. The owner's manual suggested photographing family memebers first. I remember my endless passion of photographing of my dog. Through the years, capturing nature and unsuspecting pets turned into a hobby. Our new cat, who after a year with neighbors, decided to adopt us, proved to be an especially charming, intelligent, and versatile subject. Born and educated in Poland, I have been producing radio programs on Polish music and managing the arts. This unmanageable but charming beast continues to entertain and challenge me!

TUNGILIK, TANYA

"Tarraq" means reflection of shadow in Innuinaqtun, the language of the Inuit in the Western Arctic of Canada. This photograph was taken in Cambridge Bay, Nunavut, just as I got off a twin-otter float plane. I loved the color and quality of the clouds that day, along with the mirror-like water. I love to capture photographs of landscapes and wildlife. The rest of my family are pretty good photographers as well. I hope to become a professional photographer—it is my life's passion!

TYLER, JULIE BEASLEY

I wanted to give my sister something special for Christmas, and I knew that pictures of my niece would be the way to go. Savanna was seventeen months old when I shot this picture, so I wanted to have some fun with her and the props. I placed the garland and white lights on the floor with her and added the star as we kept shooting. The baby apples and beads peaked her interest, but once the star lit up, she became entranced. When she looked down, I waited for the right time to shoot and this was just perfect. No flash was used in this picture, just the natural light from the lights and the star. This picture is a tribute to all babies that are born premature. Savanna was born at thirty-two weeks, weighing just two pounds and twelve ounces. She is our little miracle!

UHL, MARTY

This is a photograph of a summer sunset. I live in the country outside of Toledo, Ohio. The sunsets that I have taken in my backyard have been beautiful and unique. There is no sunset exactly alike. I've photographed at least 150 sunsets in the last seven years. My wife and I love the end of the day, because we know a great sunset will appear in our backyard. I really enjoy taking pictures of God's creations.

UNDERWOOD, SUMMER MAE

While studying photography at the Maryland Institute College of Arts, I discovered my love for landscape photography. I draw inspiration from Ansel Adams, William Henry Jackson, and A. Aubrey Bodine. After hiking to the top of the falls, I created this photo by balancing my tripod on two rocks, using a long exposure to capture the moment. Cunningham Falls, a seventy-eight-foot cascading waterfall, is located in the Catoctin Mountains near Thurmont, Maryland. I always carry my camera gear when hiking or mountain biking because you never know when a photographic opportunity may present itself.

VAN ARKEL, SARA LOUISE

This is a photo of the Credit River in Cheltenham, Ontario, Canada. It is just a reminder that beauty is all around us; we just have to open our eyes and look around.

VAN LEISHOUT, KARL E.

My father, Raven Van Leishout, is a prominent horticulturist in my hometown, and predictably, his property is a botanist's dream. I took this photograph next to my bedroom a few months after purchasing my first ever camera! Today, I will readily admit that I have developed a healthy appreciation for a photographer's skill and patience behind the lens, and take great pleasure in flipping through my own and others' best work. A picture may indeed say a thousand words, but no writer has ever used a thousand words to move an audience the way an ingenious photograph can.

VAN ZYL, DEAN ANDREW

This photo was taken in my front yard one afternoon. The warm light seemed to illuminate this flower so perfectly. It displays the simple beauty of God's creation! This particular shot was surprisingly taken on my compact rather than my DSLR camera.

VANDEUSEN, CAROLE C.

This photo is of my house rabbits, Zenith and Kibbles. Most people do not understand what wonderful house pets rabbits make. Zenith was a discarded Easter rabbit; now she is a wonderful Christmas bunny.

VASQUEZ, KRISTINE MARIE

I had only recent started taking up photography in my school, Father Patrick Mercredo High School in Fort McMurray, Alberta when I took "Northern Lights From My Bedroom." It was my first time to have ever seen the wonderful display of natural lights, and I got so excited. I grabbed my camera, took the picture as my teacher, Mrs. Price Chambrinho, taught me, and was quite surprised with the result. At sixteen, I was quite proud to have taken such an amazing photograph of something quite rare. And what's more amazing was that I took the picture from my bedroom. This photograph is something I'm absolutely proud of, and I'm glad to have had the opportunity to share it with others.

VASQUEZ, RICARDO

This photograph is a picture of the White House that I took in June of 2007. It was taken from the Jefferson Memorial, and I really like how the water is shown in the picture. I consider it an honor that my picture was chosen and is published among all of these other photos.

VASSALLO, TARA SAVINA

This is a photograph of my grandmother's cat, Buckwheat. I caught him laying on the dryer trying to keep warm on a cold, winter day. My grandmother asked me to take a picture of him. I was surprised how well it turned out, and the picture has been a favorite in the family.

VAUGHN, STACEY LEANA

This beach is one of my favorite spots to shoot. I was actually shooting another subject when I noticed my daughter, Hailey, was upset because I hadn't taken any pictures of her. I snapped this quickly before she was off and running again.

VENKATARAMANA, ANITA B.

This photograph was taken on a bicycling vacation. The morning sunrise glorified the basin. The scene was breathtaking. The photograph says it all.

VEROLINE, CINDY LYNN

This photo was taken after a heavy spring rain. This very spot was where my daughter and her fiancé planned to build a home. She passed away in July of 2005. This picture was taken by me during spring of 2006. It's her way of letting me know that God loves me, "So smile, Momma."

VONGPHOUTHONE, SIENGTHONG

I am an emergency nurse in Milwaukee, Wisconsin. My family and I arrived to the United States in 1989 from Laos for a better future, better economy, and a better life for ourselves. This picture reminds me of what America is about; freedom, unity, and a better future.

WADE, JASON EDWARD HORACE

This photo was one of the first I shot with a decade-old Minolta 35mm camera. It is of Chris Hunter at Raceway Park in Old Bridge Township in New Jersey. It's funny because before this photo, I never took many photographs. This photo is one of my favorites and one of the reasons I continue to take photos.

WAIT, JOSHUA J. C.

Some moments come into view and disappear quickly—a boat rocking in the water, sunsets, a child laughing, and flowers blooming in all their glory. Capturing these moments enriches my life, the lives of the people around me, and the people with whom I have the pleasure of sharing them. This picturesque scene takes place near Bar Harbor, Maine. My wife and I had a delicious trip filled with ice cream and milkshakes during a rare heat wave in Maine.

WAITE, MARY ANN

This photo was taken at a section of the Grand Canyon last spring. Overlooking the Colorado River area below left you speechless. The colors all around were breathtaking. I truly love the outdoors. You just never know what you will see around the next bend. The beauty of the outdoors is eternal. From sunrise to sunset, stop to smell the roses and check out the next bend. Even in the desert, there is beauty. I am a housewife and mother of two beautiful daughters. If I am outside, I like to have a camera around. I also work outside the home as a sales associate at ACE Hardware. I love life itself and the beauty of it all.

WALKER, BENJAMIN PARKS

This photograph was captured on a crisp, autumn afternoon. While my friend, Bob, and I were out at the historic Conrad Mansion, I happened to stumble upon a rather delicate and beautiful flower. I brandished my Nikon N90 film and captured the shot using a Tamron 300mm macro lens. I am only seventeen, but if I were to offer any sort of advice, it would be one should not overlook the ordinary or repel from the obvious. One must take something ordinary and turn it into something emotionally powerful. I feel that is what makes a true photographer.

WALKER, NIKKI LYNN

I took this photograph of myself—I just put my camera on my tripod. I do this all the time. It was for my friends. I am thirty-four and have a seventeen-year-old daughter, Alyssa. I am in nursing. I work in a nursing home and I love my residents—they are my life! The expression on my face shows how blessed I feel for being able to help people who can't help themselves.

WALKER, STACEY
I just wanted to show off my grandson, Travon, as he likes to be the center of attention. He loves cell phones just like his mother, Melissa Collins.

WALLACE, MAGGIE MAE
This picture was taken in Virginia along Skyline Drive on October 28, 2007. The leaves along most of the drive were still green, which was disappointing, but at Big Meadows, the leaves were changing colors and the low-lying brush that covers the meadows had turned red and orange, almost as though the meadow had caught on fire. Of all the views and overlooks along Skyline Drive, this was my favorite.

WARD, DEANNA LYNN
Last summer we were out at our cabin northwest of Grande Prairie, Alberta, and I noticed a beautiful butterfly floating around near the trees, so I grabbed my camera and followed it around for awhile. It finally settled onto a bush and I was able to capture it on film. I was surprised that it sat so still. Later that day, I was able to take numerous pictures of other butterflies as well. It was a very humid day, so perhaps that is why they were so abundant! Maybe next year I'll enter one of the other butterfly pictures!

WASIM, HAIDER QUAZI
By walking through the beach, I got this amazing shot of these two seagulls. It seems like they are astonished at the beauty of the sea. Watching these birds very often, I get to know interesting and funny characteristics of these sea birds. They cross through the road by walking, instead of using their wings to fly! Mother Nature always opens the door of her never-ending treasure of beauty, but we can save only a few of these precious moments in our memories.

WATSON, MICHELLE RENEA
I am eighteen years old and for as long as I can remember, I've always had a love for photography. I constantly carry my camera with me because I like to find the beauty in everything. But this picture was simply taken at my house of one of the ornaments on our Christmas tree decorated by my family and me. Finding the beauty in this certainly wasn't hard.

WEBBER, BRITTANY
I am currently studying photography at a post-secondary institution and this is just one of the pictures I took for an assignment. Our puppy, Maddie, amazingly stayed still long enough for me to snap this shot of her, and thankfully, it turned out great. I love to capture little moments like this on film and try to always have my camera ready for that special shot.

WECKSTEIN, ARIANA DENEVI
People fascinate me, and this was one of those rare moments in which I was able to capture a person's soul in a photo. I don't know this man's name or where he is now, but I know that in that moment, there was beauty on Venice Beach.

WEIGEL, BETH
I took this photo of our Collie and Golden Retiever in Wyoming. We were there on business and our Texas dogs had never seen snow. We had just adopted the Golden Retriever three days before, so she was more reluctant. They both decided they loved snow. I have been interested in photography for thirty-five years. I worked as a retoucher in a photo studio and a photo lab. My husband and I now work in the oil industry. When I look at something, I always visualize a frame around it. I have my camera ready at all times. Thank you so much for giving me the honor for my work. Friends and family have always enjoyed my work more than the camera in their face, but to be honored in this way is very special.

WELCH, SANDRA LEE
I have been interested in photography since I was about eight years old. I was fascinated by the fact you could take a picture and look at it years later and remember details surrounding the event. I am always on the lookout for the perfect picture to capture and record. Almost all of my best pictures seem to be by accident, and my planned ones are not always as good. This is a wonderful hobby for me as well as a challenge.

WELLS, SANDY ALLYNE
This picture is just of the beautiful sights I enjoy every day. There is a picture in everything. I live in the Okanagan and love being outdoors. I am excited to see one of my pictures in your book and hope there are more opportunities to come.

WERTHER, MATTHEW ALLEN
Photography has always been my passion. I love everything about it—taking pictures, looking at pictures, and I dream of building my own photography company. "Sunset Beach" was taken when I was walking on the beach at Pensacola Naval Air Station while I was there receiving some air force training. This is the firt time I have submitted a photograph and the first time I've had one published, and I would like to thank everyone who has supported my photography.

WETTSTEIN, NATAN
One day as I was working on my photo project, I took a walk through the woods to get a good nature shot. It had rained the day before, so naturally, things were wet. I stopped to look at this branch and envisioned it in sepia, and I took a quick photo.

WHITE, CAROLE ELIZABETH
I have never entered a photography contest before as a novice of photography. To say that I am stunned and overwhelmed that my photo has got this far is an understatement. This photograph is very special to me as this little beauty was lost to me when he was only ten months old with cancer. I will make this a lovely, fitting tribute to my "Purrfect" little man.

WHITE, WILLIAM GEORGE
On a Caribbean cruise calling at Antigua, the scene was set for this photo. I live in Sheringham, United Kingdom I am a heavy goods vehicle engineer. I am a member of the Sheringham R.N.L. I always have my camera with me as you never know what opportunities arise. As my wife and I cruise at least once a year, who knows what opportunities there may be for more pictures?

WHITELEY, DIANA L.
This photo was taken on a beautiful June morning in Assisi, Italy. I was traveling and touring Europe with my Aunt Glennietta and my two daughters, Jennifer and Marianne. As we entered the city, we could hear the squeals of laughter and the joyful voices of children playing. We were delighted to stop and watch them play. My aunt and I are both teachers, and we felt that this moment was such a gift as we watched these beautiful children playing and having such a good time. The "Simon says" game was played on the steps of the Basilica di Santa Chiara, and I thought that it was a beautiful moment in time to see these young ones enjoying themselves in such an old and sacred setting.

WILLIAMS, DEBRA
This is our Coco. He's our sun worshipper. We live on the coast in Half Moon Bay, California. On sunny days you will find him in all the sunny spots throughout the house, which starts on the dining room table, to the living room floor, on to the kitchen window sill, and all spread out on the kitchen floor for the last bit of sunshine. I really love taking pictures of my animals, they are such characters. My husband laughs at all the pictures I have, but to me a picture taken is a moment of delight that you will cherish forever.

WILLIAMS, DEMETRIUS M.
I never knew I had an eye for taking pictures. Thank you for recognizing my hidden talent. I appreciate the opportunity for the exposure of my beautiful photo.

WILSON, TRACEY LYNNETTE
This is a photo of our "Boopbah," Taylor Simone. This picture reminds me of how much fun we had playing in the pool. My husband was with us and after two hours in the pool, Taylor was exhausted after all that kicking and splashing in her crab boat float. We proceeded to pack up and return home, and I sat Taylor Simone on the beach chair and she had this look like, "Wow, that was awesome." I had a ball so I told my husband to quickly grab the camera so that we would always have fond memories of Taylor Simone's first birthday at the pool with Mom and Dad.

WILSON, WHITNEY RAE
As a student at Grand Valley State Univesity, I am lucky to be able to attend events in the Greater Grand Rapids area. This picture is of a member of the 61 Syx Teknique breakdancing group out of Grand Rapids, Michigan. Some of our friends dance with the group and it's always fun to go out and take amateur photographs of them. I also enjoy taking candid pictures of family and friends. I feel that catching people in their true element is most fascinating.

WINSLOW, SAM BURKE
I am a Boy Scout. I love being around nature. At summer camp this past year, I spend an afternoon walking around a valley in the Blue Ridge Mountains, Virginia. I was checking out a small stream that cut through the side of the valley when I stumbled upon a few rhododendron bushes. I probably spent fifteen minutes looking at the bush and taking pictures. I got a few good shots and a

few bad ones, but this shot really stood out in my mind. I think that this picture really captured the natural beauty that is in nature.

WOLF, SARA KATHERINE
Originally, I took this photograph for my mother, Beth, for a Mother's Day gift. She loves flowers, especially lilacs. Photography has always been my favorite hobby and I'm going to college in the fall to make it a career. I call my camera, "my baby," and it truly is.

WOODLEY-CARDY, CAROLYNE M.
This photograph helped sell our house! It was taken in the fall of 2006, depicting our newly interlocked walkway, fall mums, a new urn, and the remnants of a sleeping grapevine. My husband and I shared seven wonderful years there. Henham, Ontario will also always be dear to me because it's where I had my two sons. This picture perfectly represents the beauty, color, and fruitfulness of this time in my life, which makes its publication so special. My boys are still very young and I don't have much free time; however, this acknowledgement is truly an inspiration for me to further pursue my artistic ambitions.

WRAY, DILLON JAMES
This photograph is of a firework. As I was taking photos, the camera was about to die, so I was very lucky to get the shot—not to mention how hard it is to photograph a firework and actually see it. I am a person who likes to take pictures of odd things or just ordinary things, but a different point of view. The person I admire for teaching me how to take good pictures is Mrs. Mussinan. She was my high school digital photography teacher.

WRIGHT, ROBERT STEVE
This is a picture of a mallard duck, taken as the sun was setting one fall afternoon on Lilly Creek in Sudbury, Ontario. Since receiving my first camera for my twenty-seventh birthday in 2006, I have taken many nature photographs in the Sudbury area.

YANKEY, DELORIS
I took this picture at Rocky Fork Lake, where I live. This is such a beautiful place with endless nature all around. I have my camera in my purse at all times, always ready!

YOUNG, APRIL G. I. M.
This picture always amazes me with its simple, natural beauty. Orchids have always been revered for their elegant, exotic look. Here, I have attempted to capture and convey the essence of one beautiful, perfect moment created by nature amidst mankind's concrete jungle. This particular orchid once belonged to my fiancé's grandfather. I hope to see its splendor preserved for all time. I was born, raised, and reside in Hawaii. A simple person, I enjoy nature and life's uncomplicated pleasures. I am blessed with terrific friends and family, and I want to thank them.

YOUNG, NANCY EMERY
After meeting my friend, Joel, at the Hallmark Institute of Photography, I knew I must have a portrait of this beautiful, soulful man. The shoot was difficult, especially setting up the background

and visualizing where the lights should be, but it was worth all the hard work. The pictures were priceless and have since been recognized as fine examples of quality photography.

YOUNG, TRACI LYNN
This is Missy, one of the many animals I have rescued and found new homes for over the years. I have been in the business of saving animals for seven years and Missy captured my heart and I wanted to be able to remember her forever.

ZANZIG, JENNIFER LYNN
I love taking pictures, especially pictures of things people pass by every day from a new and interesting perspective. I believe there is beauty in everything and that it is our job as photographers to capture it and share it with the world.

ZE-DUKES, CARLOS EZEKIEL
This is a picture of my great son-in-law, "Zebra-Knight," a.k.a. Carlos E. Ze-Dukes, an international percussionist who has toured with Ray Charles. My adopted daughter, Maria R. Ze-Dukes, was the make up artist. The photo was shot in the farm's studio. I am ninety-one years young, born in 1916! I have taken the pleasure in capturing wedding photography for forty years-plus! As old as I am, I feel eternally young when I take photos. I never knew this picture was submitted until I got the letter from my son-in-law! "You've never too old or bold to photograph what's never been seen, or capture someone or thing so unique." God bless all those who love and live the life of a photographer.

ZELLER, TESSA ANN
I took this photo of my niece, Faith, in our backyard during early summer. She was restless and wanted to be outside. It was a spur-of-the-moment snapshot of her in her bare feet playing. I live in a rural village in the Finger Lakes of New York, where we are surrounded by three beautiful lakes and many Mennonite farms. I took a photography class at Finger Lakes Community College, where my instructor helped me to develop my eye for unique perspective. I enjoy taking photos and I am known to my family as "snap-happy" with the camera.

INDEX OF PHOTOGRAPHERS

A

Ackerman, Janet L.   5
Ackerson, Brandy Sue   35
Adam, Bridget K.   130
Adams, Ben   81
Adams, Bryce Richardson   116
Adams, Cherita Ann   77
Adams, Meshel Lynn   129
Adams, Sandra L.   216
Agard, Mallory Jean   152
Ahmed, Aleena Farah   232
Aiello, Leslie   48
Alcaraz, Andy Anthony   1
Alexander, Cadell L.   118
Alhomedan, Fowzya A.   124
Allen, Dori   240
Amador, Guillermo Enrique   31
Anacleto, Evangeline Gaudiosa   76
Anderson, Ashley Ann   60
Anderson, Chelsey Rae   5
Anderson, Eric   39
Anderson, Sandra   177
Andrahovitch, Carly Anna   71
Angelene, Joannah   189
Angulo, Salma   239
Angus, Laura L.   137
Ankney, Desirae Lynn   204
Anthony, Beth   168
Anthony, Randi Amber   107
Archibald, Shenelle Rose   181
Arel, Cristin   182
Arender, Karen Ann   73
Arion, Lisa Beth   68
Armstrong, Susan Gayle   7
Arnett, Autumn Mariya   240
Arnold, Dale   111
Arnold, Mark Reid   132
Arthur, Charlotte Jane   164
Arturo, Julie Marie   114
Arzaga, Gina K.   56
Ashby, Erica   227
Atamaniuk, Jonathan Ashley   84
Atkinson, Aaron James   66
Atterberry, Bernadette M.   232
Autrey, Jackie   19
Avello, Jennifer Nicole   136
Avendano-Quinones, Ingrid   111
Avery, Bill D.   139
Ayala, Nickki L.   142

B

Baines, Devon Montgomery   171
Baker, Debbie Lynn   128
Baker, Joan   35
Baker, Patrick Anthony   12
Baldwin, Donald   112
Baldwin, Kelly Maire   164
Baltz, Charles Wayne   224
Banker, Benjamin D.   67
Barker, Sheryl L.   240
Barnes, Meredith Ellen   149
Barnes, Zanetta A.   27
Barr, Elizabeth Robin   146
Bartelt, Bernd   19
Basha, Farida N.   50
Bass, John Clifford, Sr.   159
Batista, Judith Nilsa   223
Baxter, Jeannette Maryanne   64
Bean, Taylor Lynn   135
Bearden, Brad Jay   137

Beasley, Jared Michael   126
Beaton, Madeleine Rose   80
Beaudoin, Elaine   57
Beckman, Tammy Elizabeth   46
Beckman, Tina   32
Beesley, Sheridan Hastings   218
Beganovic, Mladen   6
Begg, Donald John   86
Beland, Rick   175
Belcher, Yvette   217
Belenky, Yuliya   131
Beletskaya, Maryana   60
Bell, Shelly May   104
Bellavance, Benjamin Eric   27
Bendall, Samuel Wren   46
Benner, Mark Alan   51
Bennett, Jane Laura   85
Benoit, Chelsea T.   164
Benson, Jeannie M.   46
Bergstrom, Susann   22
Bergum, Whitney Jean   63
Bermudez, Jennifer L.   47
Bernardi-Wray, Lynda   183
Berndt, Lindsay L.   195
Bertrand, Francis Paul   158
Biancani, Peter Joseph   76
Bieth, Scott Allan   131
Bigby, Jennifer Lynn   182
Billingham, Edward Alan   128
Bilodeau, Madeleine Christine   79
Blakeley, Jackie Yvonne   186
Bloomer, Jessica Renee   26
Blostica, Brian Mathew   64
Boc, Annissa Dianne   144
Bodart, Megan   40
Boivin, Jessica Ann   177
Boling, Jason   189
Bonck, Perry J.   166
Bone, Patrick James   76
Borgerding, Trina Rose Marie   98
Bos, James J.   75
Bottone, Roseanne   143
Bouchillon, Brooke Ann   116
Boudrow, Douglas A.   3
Bowden, Randall Kohl   62
Boyd, Tammy   220
Boyer, Christa   199
Boyer, Jeff W.   206
Bradley, Tyson Ray   58
Brant, Linda L.   219
Braunlin-Stites, Katie M.   223
Britton, Patricia Gillingham   98
Brockman, Michelle Helen   32
Bromley, Holly Laurie   163
Brookes-Tsang, Rebecca Jane   142
Brookman, Amy Renee   9
Brooks, Curt James   214
Broscious, Judy   183
Brower, Mary Margaret   190
Brown, A. J.   191
Brown, Anne Mills   234
Brown, Annette   5
Brown, Geoffrey D.   30
Brown, John W.   25
Brown, Sarah K.   131
Bruce, Mark C.   185
Brucia, Eric Anthony   223
Brunner, Jodi Marie   91
Brunst, Mary Elizabeth   29
Bryan, Virginia   129
Brydie, Pamela D.   10
Buchholtz, Kristine Lynn   41
Buhoci, Caterina   172

Bujold, Noella   79
Buliani, Stefano   78
Bull, Michael Robert   56
Buller, Haley   214
Bullock, Caitlin Shay   189
Bumgardner, Ashley Marie   226
Bunda, Karen Lynn   65
Burchfield, Charlesty Misty   26
Burden, Sara Lee   148
Burdick, Jennifer Susan   30
Burnett, Kaitlyn E.   6
Burns, Simon Parnell   157
Burris, Hal   13
Burt, Ann Marie   86
Burton, Chelsea Grace   9
Burton, Rebecca Anne   70
Bush, April   138
Bush, Connie S.   197
Busing, Heather A.   39
Bustos, Liliana   247
Butler, Mike   143
Buxar, Teresia Jana   126

C

Cabral, Chase Anthony   2
Cacioppo, Eleanor Caroline   200
Calam, Melonie Anne   63
Calcaterra, Megan Leigh   20
Calhoun, Alexis Briana   152
Calvelage, Charissa Ann   176
Calvert, Shirley Louise   192
Campa, Michael Allen   133
Campbell, Trey   141
Capparelli, John M.   229
Carey, Katie A.   149
Caro, Susan   196
Carr, Kathy A.   100
Cash, Scottye J.   176
Castro, Michelle Marie   175
Catron, Salena M.   124
Catron, Thomas R.   78
Caulfield, Cindy Lynn   35
Ceravino, Claire   228
Chaffee, Cory   151
Chalmers, Anna Nadine   204
Chancheck, Imeleta Tatiana   88
Chaney, Greg A.   82
Chapman, Adam Grant   14
Chapman, Amy Marie   51
Chastain, Emily Elizabeth   243
Cheng, Andrew Ka Ho   71
Chilcott, Linda Rose   58
Chirico, Dina Ann   83
Chislett, Neil Clive   116
Chiu, Cassaundra E.   69
Cho, Haewon   113
Choudhury, Farhana S.   219
Christensen, Kayla Rae   142
Christiansen, Bree Celeste   52
Christoffersen, Lee Gordon   187
Christy, Lawrence David   231
Chu, Richard L.   3
Ciesienski, Anya Alyssa   84
Claborn, Shanna Lynn   59
Clark, Ken J.   68
Clark, Patricia Carol   139
Clarke, Kaye Alison   96
Clawson, Michael Paul   47
Clay, Brad James   106
Clem, Daniel Scott   192
Clemens, Shelbi D.   155

Clifford, Ben George   111
Clisby, Loressa Anita   145
Cloutier, Michael   74
Coats, Michael   22
Coe, Sandra   184
Coers, Erica Lynn   234
Coffin, Courtney Marie   112
Cogburn, Donita   198
Collard, Joanne Beverly   53
Collette, Jaymie   234
Collins, Christopher O'Neal   16
Collins, Jo Ann   97
Collison, Stacey Breanne   109
Colon, Olga Maria   242
Colton, Lauren Elizabeth   182
Conn, Patrick William   13
Connolly, Jesse James   81
Considder, Bryan Michael   119
Cook, Martine Ann   237
Cook, Nicholas Johnathan   155
Cook, William LeRoy   171
Cool, Dean S.   129
Coon, Jenna M.   53
Cooper, June Rader   205
Cooper, Scott T. E.   82
Corby, Tina Louise   50
Cordeiro, Kim C.   94
Corsetto, Amy Beth   13
Costa, Trish   178
Cotter, Nadia   181
Cottone, Dana Marie   220
Courns, Zara Ellen   242
Coursolle, Carrie Ann   77
Cowie, William Arthur   141
Cox, Amy M.   68
Cox, Erin Elizabeth   58
Coy-Stout, Victoria Lynn   207
Crabtree, Tracy L.   162
Crane, Suzanne Gail   34
Crary, John Rollie   241
Crawford, Blandye J.   96
Crawford, Savannah Tinsley   246
Creurer, Paul Daniel   72
Crews, Randall Jay   134
Crimmins, Wendy L.   227
Criswell, Bobby D.   32
Crneckiy, Nick   70
Crooks, Matthew Brian   107
Croshier, Carrie Rose   179
Crosley, Dan Alan   19
Crouch, Linda Charlene   102
Crouch, Matthew   141
Crowther, Lisa-May   65
Crutchfield, Jonna   3
Cruz, Luisa   54
Cudahy, Laurie   88
Cullen, Timothy James   220
Cunningham, Molly Joy   51
Cunningham, Morris   83
Cunningham, Samantha   186
Curran, Colleen Margaret   108
Curtis, Nichole Marie   160

D

D'amours, Diane   179
D'Andrea, Sonia Rose   174
D'Orazio, Laura E.   227
Daia, Marcel   218
Dale, Andy   19
Daley, John A.   204

Dalton, Keighla Marie   132
Daly, Laura Elizabeth   222
Daniels, Claire Gay   153
Daniels, Teresa Ann   69
Dappen, Alex   28
Darnell, Pearce David   122
Davidson, Kenna R.   172
Davies, Olamide   238
Davis, Chantal Mary   96
Davis, Kendra May   45
Davis, Vicky Jo   148
Davis, William Thomas, Sr.   138
Dawson, Jimmy   211
De Virgilio, Maria Paula   183
Dean, Kelly L.   135
Deardurff, Sarah Elaine   125
Dedona, Roseanne   220
DeHaven, Christopher Ryan   243
Deis, Betsy Knapp   122
Dejacomo, Clare Terry   15
Delaney, Bill   208
DeLauder, Sherry Anne   140
DeLeal, Angela G.   52
Delesbore, Sharon Juanita   239
Delozier, Meghan Grace   14
Deltcheva, Iliana G.   181
Demars, Darlene Ann   94
Demas, Julie A.   85
Demboski, James Michael   69
Dennis, Kathy Lynn   22
Deon, Eugenie Marie   166
Deon, Tuesday Ann   173
Depasse, Emily   117
Desjean, Jessica Paige   218
Devine, Ashley Payge   88
Dewell, Kristie Ann   22
DeWindt, Krissy   213
Diana, Alexandra Angelica   163
Dilk, Danyell A.   184
Dill, Leelah Dawn   155
Dillard, Amanda Kate   35
Dilley, Alex Orlove   93
Dimattia, Joe   79
DiPalma, Angela Marie   235
Disher, Tara-Lynn   205
Docherty, Lisa Lynn   191
Doerfler, Marisa Ann   17
Donges, Jaclyn Beth   25
Donilon, Joseph C.   33
Dorman, Mel   191
Dowling, Marilyn Ann   69
Downey, Nicole L.   2
Drew, Nicole Lee   105
Drozdyk, Kim Carole   56
Druien, Alex C.   9
Duff, Erin Leigh   61
Duggan, Jarrad   105
Dumford, Aaron J.   197
Duncan, Erica Noelle   150
Dunevant, Jennifer Lane   198
Dunlop, Lindsay Susan   155
Dunn, Bridget   176
Dunn, Norm   99
Dunnington, Earl Victor, Jr.   187
Dutton, Thomas Watson   12

E

Eanes, Megan Leigh   144
Eash, Terri W.   113
Easterly, Sarah   5
Edgett, Deb J.   221

Edgington, Barbara Hale   194
Edwards, Sonja Michele   49
Eicher, Doug   210
Elder, Angie   17
Eldred, Tara Louise   64
Ellenberger, Linda   99
Ellis, Wendy Jo   71
Emerson, Challaine Morgan   56
Emmerson, Leah Jade   78
Emon, Tammy Denise   91
Engel, Lis   223
Enriquez, Carl   21
Esneault, Suzette Marie   190
Esposito, Lisa Anne   132
Esteban, Suwela   176
Evans, Ashley Elizabeth   226
Exarhos, Heather D.   222
Eyrich, Peter J.   93
Ezerins, Dillon John   233

F

Fafard, Kina L.   171
Fain, Stacie Lynn   142
Fairbrun, Grant E.   40
Fairchild, Christina M.   247
Falconieri, David W.   77
Falgout, Rachel Concetta   158
Falsetti, Kayla Dawn   232
Farley, Megan Lynn   221
Farnham, Allen   27
Farnham, Allen J.   127
Faro, Rose   111
Feldstein, Michael   169
Ferenc, Jill Melanie   20
Ferguson, Candy Sue   105
Ferko, Jackie   47
Fernandez, Arturo R.   119
Fiander, Joan   117
Fields, Lisa Rayel   31
Fillman, Heather Lynn   180
Finch, Augustina   106
Finch, Channing Brianne   246
Fisher, Cheryl D.   94
Fisher, Paul John   227
Fleck, Jennifer Rebecka   246
Fletcher, Karen   64
Flinn, Krista S.   232
Flores, Consuelo M.   199
Floyd, Seth James   94
Flury, Kathi   18
Foderaro, Andrew   245
Foglesong, Pamela Lynn   130
Foley, Toni Ann   152
Fonnest, Bruce Wayne   125
Fontana, Giovanni   52
Fontenot, Cathy Marie   24
Ford, Orren   130
Foreman, Marcia K.   68
Forrest, Keith W.   94
Foster, Steve   162
Frakes, Zane R.   215
Franck, Elizabeth Jo   221
Francoeur, Charlotte A.   223
Frank, Brian S.   96
Frankham, Cassandra Leigh   105
Franz, Anna Rebekah   192
Freed, Richard   235
Freedman, Joshua   91
Freeman, Kaitlin Danone   3
Fridrich, Christian K.   196
Frost-Smith, Kaye Elizabeth   100

Fulk, Brenda L.   178
Fullen, Sandy Dee   72
Fuqua, Dulcey H.   67
Furgason, Gloria Jean   58
Furness, Judith Mary-Alice   167

G

Gache, Rio M.   215
Gadd, Jerry L.   34
Gaeta, Louis James   9
Gagne, Isabel   150
Gallagher, T. J.   2
Gallaway, Jaime Sue   245
Gamotis, Glenn Albert   209
Gandalone, Alyse Nichole   144
Ganje, Candace Lee   189
Garcia, Amy Jill   229
Gardiner, Melissa Mae   80
Gardner, Paul Bradford   180
Gardner, Tonya A.   137
Garibay, Lourdes   95
Garner, Joshua B.   64
Garvin, Cindy B.   192
Gati, Carrie J.   98
Gatling, Stacy Jeanne   4
Gaudet, Donna   205
Gauthier, Rachelle   87
Gemmell, Harry Robert James   206
Gerard, Rosemarie Ann   183
Geraud, Maurice Fred   201
Gerber, Juan   157
Gerin, Patricia Ann   171
Geritz, Marie   121
Gerrish, Jessica L.   59
Gethers, Khadijah   154
Gharios, Karim Pierre   44
Gianfalla, Melissa Ann   26
Gibney, Sandra Michelle   174
Gillis, Matthew Daniel   196
Gilmore, Vivian Leigh   85
Gladden, Robert Dale   30
Glass, Andrea Katherine   130
Golea, Vince   108
Goodyk, Monte   18
Gorman, Ida N.   145
Gorski, Shane   197
Gould-May, Jerico Rochelle   235
Graham, Jamie Lee   80
Grandmaison, Pam June   131
Granger, Brenda   5
Grausam, Tanya   154
Gray, Krystal Dawn   54
Gray-Faude, Pamela Ann   184
Green, Loyce Leslie   243
Green, Melissa   35
Green, Paul Terence   72
Gregersen, Tabatha Ann   148
Grein, Shaun Perry   77
Grenier, Carol   99
Gresens, William A.   197
Greve, Elizabeth   174
Grieve, Caitlin Patricia   25
Griffin, William C.   174
Grossman, Jo   54
Grosso, Lindsay Elizabeth   123
Gruenloh, Amanda Katherine   77
Guajardo, Amanda   173
Gudmundson, Wendy   66
Gul, Pelin   103
Gurino, Cynthia P.   4
Guth, James Alan   38

Guzman, Jaime E.   100
Guzman, Tierra Noelle   221

H

Haake, Erik Anders Michael   93
Haberl, Joseph Hart   41
Hagedus, Michele   74
Hajek, Barbara B.   86
Haley, Alan J.   115
Haley, Ross Sublett   8
Hall, Sara Faye   104
Halliburton, Jason Vladinir   65
Hamersly, Katherine Ann   224
Hamilton, Kelsey Jaye   21
Hamilton, Krista Ann   149
Hammill, Jaci Elizabeth   45
Haner, Clayton   107
Hankin, Elaine E.   206
Hanlon, Maddie Alexandra   154
Hansen, Missy Kay   23
Hanson, Andy M.   42
Hardesty, Tracey J.   104
Harmon, Barbara Ann   247
Harper, Jessica Dawn   140
Harper, Rebecca Lynn   63
Harper, Whitney Nicole   101
Hart, Thomas W.   133
Hart, Valerie Jean   220
Hartman, Jennifer Nicole   208
Hartstang, Nick   3
Haskett, Catherine M.   38
Hatfield, Joshua Dean   17
Hattermann, Troy Alan   73
Hatton, Ronald J.   90
Hauser, April A.   218
Hawkins, Corrina Pam   136
Hay, John Luke   135
Hayes, Louise   182
Hays, Kristin Suzanne   198
Hearndon, Donna Gail   28
Hedgspeth, Joelle Ann   247
Heidenheim, Suzanne   159
Heintz, Jenny Lynn   200
Helgerson, Abbie Lyn   158
Helland, Sydney K.   41
Hemsworth, Linda Jean   81
Henderson, Krystal Marie   57
Henderson, Michelle Ann   81
Hendricks, Kelsie Ann   147
Hendrix, Angie V.   120
Henkell, Mark L.   153
Herbert, Chelsea Brienna   110
Hernandez, Vanessa Lara   55
Herndon, Cynthia Marie   106
Herrera, Alex   241
Hersey, Nicholas Alonzo   82
Hersom, Hamie C.   225
Hertel, Tiffany Lazette   23
Hicker, Kolya Nicolay   107
Higginbotham, Sherri   51
Hill, Lynn   188
Hill, Rachel Marie   42
Hine, Michael   19
Hittel, Austin Robert   19
Hoekenga, Debra   212
Hoets, Leigh-Ann Chase   50
Hoisington, Kerry   90
Hokaszewski, Jessica Rose   192
Hollenbach, Janet Rose   11
Holloway, Jon   156
Holmes, Tracy Darlene   173

Holt, Emma Louise   70
Homer, Candee M.   246
Hoofman, Brittlynn Rose   17
Hoppa, Brittney   25
Horst, Judy Nicole   154
Hoskins, Mike David   120
Hostetler, Diane Kay   18
Houle, David Eric   162
Houser, Alexis A.   123
Howard, Adam N.   109
Huff, Sarah Christine   63
Hughes, Charles Michael   100
Hughes, Georgia Kay   149
Hughes, Whitney   118
Hunlin, Shelley Ann   42
Hunt, Alison H.   81
Hunt, Andrew Aaron   119
Hurd, Jessica Lynn   201
Hurley, Stacie Elizabeth   186
Hurrle, Kimberly Marie   240
Hyatt, Alison   29

I

Ibragimov, Jaqueline   128
Ilagan, Alan Bennett   7
Ilchyna, Breanne Lee   116
Iliyn, David James   11
Ipsen, Laurie   126
Irvin, Caitlyn Rebecca   153
Isakson, Emily Ann   37
Ito, Elizabeth Blanche   26
Ivanoskos, Paula Terese   210
Ivelja, Juliana Lucia   16
Izzard, Barbara   211

J

Jablonski, Rebecca Ann   159
Jacimore, Heather E.   165
Jackson, Christopher   62
Jackson, Susan D.   146
Jacobs, Alicia Marie   163
Jacobson, Saskia Quinn   63
Jarvis, Hannah   117
Jeffries, Beth R.   121
Jenkins, Bennie P.   143
Jenkins, John Spencer   10
Jenkins, Tara   95
Jenkins, Tom   195
Jensen, Sherron Swapp   195
Jerinic, Boki   88
Jilks, Kimberly Marie   201
Jobson, Jody Lynn   45
Joca, Tami A.   187
Johansen, Belinda Jane   181
Johnsgaard, Brailyn Tyrell   155
Johnson, Celena   154
Johnson, Corey D.   85
Johnson, Courtney Marie   215
Johnson, Don Roy   155
Johnson, Douglas   58
Johnson, Jamie Elizabeth   245
Johnson, Joann   163
Johnson, Joseph Daniel   20
Johnson, Kayla Raye   144
Johnson, Lindsey Kristine   107
Johnson, Marvin E.   236
Johnson, Ryan Harrison   187
Johnson-Garrard, Desiree Star   52
Johnston, Blair Tyler   120

Johnston, Emily Maureen   164
Johnston, Jessica Marie   98
Johnston, Joel Eli   50
Johnston, Robert P.   59
Johnston, Steve Martin   178
Jones, Andre   107
Jones, Angel Leah   43
Jones, Brenda Kay   237
Jones, Gaynor   121
Jones, Kathleen M.   53
Jones, Stephanie Lydie   78
Jones, Steve   15
Jordan, Julie Anne   227
Jordan, Liz   196
Jose, Allana Lynne   125
Joseph, Stefanie A.   25
Joshi, Rekha   92
Joyce, Dani   148
Jung, Kumseok   164

K

K., Beth   235
Kabas, Jonathan Jason   61
Kalafut, Cecille H.   168
Kandinova, Alina   90
Kane, Lora H.   112
Kang, Katheleen   129
Karikis, Kim   193
Karn, Jaymie Silken   93
Karn, Wesley Adam   156
Karpinski, Charles Henry   15
Kazamer, Pam K.   32
Kearse, Cyndi Ann   145
Keever, Holly Rene   182
Kelley, Sharon Lynn   199
Kelly, John   193
Kelly, Michael-Francis   81
Kelly, Shannan   237
Kendrick, Jenna M.   76
Kennedy, Darcy   89
Kennedy, Jay   126
Kennedy, Kaylin Krystal   138
Kenny, Michael David   36
Kent, Hannah Rebekah   149
Kevser   13
Khan, Jennifer   226
Khanna, Kajoli   113
Kidd, Samantha Brittany   174
Kidd, Tosha Ann   82
Kim, Seung Woo   11
Kimball, Traci L.   135
Kindt, Robyn   134
King, Becky Toccoa   122
King, Gregory Allen   105
King, Nechola Antoinette   227
Kingsbury, Joy   86
Kiniry, Debi J.   225
Kirkland, Michelle E.   74
Kirkland, Yvette   4
Kivell, Ashlee Amanda   99
Kling, Cheyenne A.   244
Kneeland, Les J.   171
Knepp, Diane Marie   46
Knoblauch, Kristi Ann   18
Kohler, Dion L., Sr.   217
Kongkham, Paul   183
Konikow, Amber Lee   118
Koon, Maria Victoria   59
Koprivech, Amanda Jane   229
Kossan, Kelley   151
Kossitch, John   55

Koster, Peter   213
Kowalick, Noelle   197
Koyne, Carol J.   139
Kozak, Cary   147
Kramer, Evan Thomas   8
Kranick, Beth   18
Kreefer, Kristen Leigh   49
Krueger, Arthur H.   99
Krueger, Tamara   37
Krueger, Timothy C.   143
Kruger, Wayanne Mae   222
Kruse, Deborah A.   217
Kuehn, Richard M.   241
Kummer, Debora Lynn   69
Kunkel, Paul Chris   160
Kunstek, Louis William   62
Kyle, Elizabeth S.   215
Kytlica, Nichole E.   21

L

La Bruyere, J. P. Edward   17
Lacroix, Patrick   188
LaFrance, Kenneth Lee   72
Laird, Mary-Kate   10
Lamm, Alison H.   28
Lamont, Grant   55
Lane, Mark Joseph   93
Laruccia, Michelle Maree   198
Lascasas, Kayla Alexandra   168
Latham, Jake Wolseley   115
Lauro, Lawrence   187
Lauser, Mandi G.   61
Laverty, James Bradley   1
Lavoie, Olivier   168
Law, Amanda Leigh   208
Law, Liz M.   23
Lawrence, Mallory Rae   132
Lax, Leo   5
Layng, Simon James   109
Lazore, Crystal Joy   231
Leahy, Sarah Eve   226
Leal, Darleen   234
LeClair, Carrie L.   15
Lee, Godwine   164
Lefferts, Jacob R., III   194
Leiserson, David Avery   29
Lelkes, Ilonka   179
Lemke, Nicole M.   83
Lemons, Darrin   211
Leon, Mischa D.   122
Levine, Rikki Erin   38
Lewallen, Megan Marie   159
Li, Michael   50
Lichtenstein, Daniel Samuel   148
Likens, Misty Ann   10
Lilley, Melissa Ann   162
Lilly, Rachel Randall   75
Limbaugh, DeLacey Amber   217
Lindsay, Jim W.   61
Litourneau, Theresa E.   182
Lloyd, Arthur Christopher   200
Lohman, Amy Lauren   101
Long, Abigail Marie   238
Long, James Wyatt   167
Long, Sandy Nanod   65
Long, Vicky I.   86
Longnecker, Kristen Nicole   14
Lopardo, Karoline   177
Loren, Michelle   219
Lorenz, Linda Dian   230
Loth, Sky Alice   91

Lovejoy-Welch, Barbara Jean   203
Lucente, Stephanie Alexandra   39
Lucosky, Tara Beth   87
Luong, Jessica   214
Lutman, Cheryl   90
Lutz, Joshua Mark   76
Luvera, Kate   45
Ly, Mike   201
Lyles, Harry Troise   212
Lyles, Jeff   178
Lyman, Jennifer   125
Lynn, Brandi   120
Lyons, Hajnalka Timea   134
Lywood, Toby Gifford   169

M

Maas, John Edward   194
Mabe, Michael Douglas   140
Mabe, Tracey Alice   191
Mabon, Louise Kathleen   75
Mabra, Rebecca E.   16
MacDougall, Mary Doris   102
Mach, Jordon Adidas   34
Mahoney, Sharon L.   151
Maier, Dawn   42
Majerovsky, Sasha   225
Mallen, Brenton John   48
Malone, Kim   48
Mangrum, Carlon Porche   33
Mannes, Whitney P.   230
Manville, Kirsten Michela   205
Marang, Jerry Scott   157
Marcapura, Erika Rossio   124
Marczynski, Oscar   193
Marie, Rita J.   128
Mario, Brittany Lyn   48
Markel, Stephanie Rita-Anne   103
Marks, Hollie Dawn   110
Marlowe, Raeleen   21
Marris-Walker, Jennifer K.   207
Marsh, Tom C.   211
Marshall, Frederick   208
Marshall, Melinda Karen   36
Martin, Dennis Patrick   225
Martin, Emily Anne   140
Martin, Lisa Rena'   244
Martin, Sarah Nicole   96
Martinez, Bianca Amanda   137
Martinez, Eva   170
Martinez, Lorena Orozco   124
Martinez, Maritza Barbara   113
Marzullo, Anthony John   17
Mascolo, Caitlan Elizabeth   195
Mason, Daniela Elizabeth   159
Mason, Debbie Ann   12
Matchett, Jordan William   161
Matheson, Dinah   189
Mathias, Natasha Melissa   34
Mathis, Cherry Nicole   70
Matzke, Jennifer L.   133
Mayel-Afshar, Sam   180
Mayer, Whitney Leigh   44
Mazo, Michael Lee   145
McBride, Barbara L.   142
McCann, Michelle C.   150
McCarthy, Laura Susan   202
McCarty, Kelly Marie   7
McClelland, Dawn Angela   8
McCloskey, Cynthia   104
McClure, Nicole Robin   146
McClure, Vickie L.   32

McCollum, Tarryn Shea   222
McCombs, Mary Jo   152
McCoy, Bradley Derring   241
McDonald, Elizabeth S.   237
McInroy, Katie   96
McIntosh, Jennifer Anne   12
McKee, Ashley Jane   119
McKinney, Laurie Anne   239
McKinney, Patricia Lynn   136
McKlemurry, Ryleigh Paige   56
McKown, Samantha Eileen   141
McLain, Donald J.   194
McLaren, Jo-Anne Mary   178
McLaughlin, Lisa Javaras   137
McLellan, Annicia Marie   170
McMahon, Alyssa   62
McNaughton, Jennifer   74
McNeal, Willie   156
McNeil, Daniel Michael   47
McPherson, Kylie   198
Medin, Shelby Payton   80
Meeks-El, Karen E.   237
Mehrzad, Farid   208
Mellen, Yahsha Tamidah   173
Mellgren, Jeffrey Alan   109
Mendelevich, Elena   150
Meriwether, Stefani L.   120
Merriam, Carol   163
Merritt, Dorothy N.   210
Messer, Diane   234
Metcalf, Michael Bryan   39
Metsala, Kaili   108
Michael, Allison Margaret   229
Micucci, Kristan Hope   141
Mielke, Jo Anne   190
Mihalich, Megan Emily   46
Miles, Jennifer Ann   161
Milevskiy, Trevor John   28
Miller, Benjamin Stephen   229
Miller, Carole A.   224
Miller, Cornellia Kate   145
Miller, Josh P.   236
Miller, Justin Todd   12
Miller, Samantha Holly   38
Miller, Zee Loraine   235
Milliken, Brian James   38
Mills, Destiny L.   228
Milner, Shaun   236
Milton, Elizabeth Anne   24
Mirabal, Vivian Belinda   87
Mitchell, Dee D.   209
Moeller, Kaitlyn Davis   148
Mohan, Jay Patrick   83
Mohl, Adam W.   206
Monaghan, Mike James   156
Mongan, Traci Kaye   108
Monheim, Ally Marie   162
Montgomery, Deborah Ann   230
Moody, Alexis Nicole   229
Mooney, Deborah Ann   143
Moore, Danielle L.   238
Moore, Jamie Estelle   102
Moore, Marlene E.   232
Moore, Steven Lynn   152
Morales, Joseph M.   180
Morgan, Lindsey Marie   214
Mormino, Danielle N.   134
Morris, Marci Lynne   27
Mortensen, Cherie   31
Mortensen, Kenzie   207
Moto, Josh   144
Mueller, Sandy   169

Munro, Jenny   236
Murchie, Tristen R.   18
Murphy, Alexandra Simone   240
Murphy, Chadd Allan   118
Murphy, Matthew Bradon   1
Myer, Donna Foster   85
Myers, Janet   165

N

Nacaytuna, Fatima Alvinez   228
Nagle, Gayle M.   56
Nagy, A. L.   177
Nambu, Shintaro   24
Nash, Aaron Richard   139
Neace, Shelby Erin   179
Neale, James Richard   110
Neavin, Gabrielle Blair   228
Nederpelt, Warren   203
Nejman, Marjorie Ann   114
Nellis, Blake Andrew   70
Nelson, Brenda   89
Nelson, Gary   137
Nelson, Janice Marie   55
Nelson, Kenneth E.   188
Nelson, Kristi Jean   187
Neltner, Misty Marie   241
Nemarich, John Peter   147
Nemeth, Cory Jade   83
Neubacher, Michael James   139
Newberry, Tim David   88
Newman, Mary Alice   206
Newman, Michael   34
Newman, Trish   73
Newsome, Jacqueline Dawn   140
Newton, Daniel E.   67
Nguyen, Tong   49
Nicholson, Aaron Shea   16
Nicholson, Amber   184
Nicholson, Amy Mae   149
Nicholson, Pam Nicole   109
Nickhorn, Andreas   138
Nicoll, James Douglas   152
Nicotra, David Alfio   65
Nieman, Crystal Lynn   118
Nort, Gayle Van   104
Novak, Donna Marie   193

O

O'Connell, James Eugene   207
O'Donnell, Penny Anne   100
O'Dwyer, Kylee Lynn   146
O'Neill, Nicole Marie   78
O'Roark, Tara Diane   88
Ochoa, Janessa   200
Odom, Rachel Elizabeth   170
Ognjenovski, Alex Daniel   150
Ogunbamiyo, Hope   43
Okhovat, Hanieh   108
Oliveira, Ana Christina   41
Olsen, Jessie   16
Olson, Lynsey   36
Ong, Chan   133
Oramas, Erica L.   186
Ordonez, Herman   58
Orekhova-Tibbits, Svetlana G.   108
Orlando, Caroline Rose   202
Orm, Sally Ann   188
Orr, Stacey Elaine   208
Oshier, William L.   217
Oswald, Fahrinisa Fatima   13

Owen, Max L.   79
Owen, Robert R.   4
Owen, Tessa Kathleen   37
Owens, Kimberly A.   145

P

Padilla, Chantelle Rae   53
Page, Brian Kent   103
Paine, Candy Thompson   13
Palacios, Andrea   60
Palafox, Andrea   188
Palmen, Abigail Ardiles   138
Palmer, Myrtle Jean   82
Palmer, Patrick   78
Pangborn, Tom   34
Paratchek, Arianna Renee   213
Parker, Brittany Sabrina   29
Parker, Clayton L.   106
Parker, Jordan   97
Parnell, Richard Peter   156
Parrish, Brittany M.   100
Parrott, Adrianna Renae   243
Parton, Elizabeth Ann   1
Pascut, Greg   75
Pasic, Ramiz   68
Pasquariello, Melissa Ann   236
Paterson, Shannon   154
Patterson, Kevin S.   106
Patterson, Sherry   167
Pattison, Stephh Gloria   217
Patton, Annie   131
Patton, Duncan Allen   84
Payne, Julian   168
Pease, Rita Antoinette   196
Pecor, Tracy   36
Pedro, Jenn   66
Peebles, Jacqueline Anne   157
Pekar, Sara   9
Peng, Helen   66
Penner, Camille Joy   50
Penny, Judith   52
Peragine, Kevin   231
Perez, Tina M.   90
Peszek, Sandra   71
Peterson, Rachel Ann   115
Peterson, Robert Drew   124
Petrosyan, Lilit   65
Petrov, Kiril   2
Phares, Ian   166
Phelan, Christopher   123
Phelps, Heather   11
Phelps, Robert Joseph   12
Phillips, Katie Kay   139
Piantadosi, Debbie   120
Picard, Tina   51
Pickelsimer, BeLinda Lee   205
Pickering, Marty   216
Piedrahita, Catalina   40
Pierre, Jason   116
Pinkerton, Thomas   193
Piper, Jacquelyn R.   43
Platcow, Harry M.   86
Plourde, Lisa   186
Plumbly, Ken V.   89
Plummer, Sarah   35
Poddar, Varun   44
Poenitske, Janell Lynn   212
Pollard, Megan Elizabeth   49
Pollock, Laurena   241
Pool, Kayleigh Victoria   69
Poor, Antoinette Dawn   136

Pope, Sarah Nicole   49
Popova, Natalia   14
Popow, Lorrie   166
Porter, David   214
Posluszny, Richard Paul   47
Poulin, Eric   225
Poulos, Jessica   89
Powell, Bradford James   193
Prado, Margareth Lyra   14
Praino, Rossanna   127
Pranskevich, Jessica Marie   114
Prasad, Colin K.   91
Price, Nina   172
Prichard, Sarah   147
Pringle, Charlotte N.   41
Profitt, Ron L.   151
Propps, Arthur Gene, Jr.   196
Proteau, Lisa-Marie   93
Pusic, Kimberly   122
Puskas, Kitti   244
Pyle, Andrew Davis   167
Pyle, Monica Jo   135

Q

Queen, Wyatt Randall   10
Quiroga, Mauricio   234

R

Raftovich, Tara Jane   7
Rains, Lori S.   103
Rakoci, Dana Marie   61
Ralph, Tonia Marie   161
Ramaley, Katie Rose   142
Ramler, Heather S.   37
Randall, John Arthur   183
Randall, Katie Marie   161
Randazzo, Cathy L.   98
Ransome, Megan   242
Raper, Steven   32
Raposo, Michelle A.   130
Rattray, Charlotte Afonsa   99
Raught, Chad Michael   1
Ray, Angela M.   230
Read, Carissa Nicole   216
Reading, Rob   116
Redfern, Philippa   22
Redmond, Drew Pierre   126
Reese, Rich   37
Reid, Blake Lee   180
Reid, Christian McClelland   197
Reilly, William J. G.   133
Renfro, Joy Marie   233
Rew, Kearstin   222
Rice, Valerie Renee   199
Richardson, Sherri A.   112
Richardson, Tim D.   214
Richie, Diane Lynn   106
Riemer, Heinz   173
Riggs, Eugene   53
Riley, Barbara L.   26
Rink, Kasi G.   44
Ritchie, Tabitha Jayne   190
Robbs, Nicholas Floyd   22
Robillard, Kyle M.   44
Robinette-Dublin, Angelia D.   240
Robinson, Carma J.   218
Robinson, Jonathan Robert   189
Robinson, Molly Sara   127
Robinson, Russell Ellise   54
Rocheleau, Patrick George   84

Rodriguez, Melissa   121
Rodriguez, Melvin   127
Rogers, Melissa May   232
Rolfsen, Benthe Ljostad   47
Rollins, Joyce Malynda   157
Romero, Jason Ronald   89
Roomet, Erik Bentley   101
Roper, James Paul   238
Rosario, Sonia   210
Ross, Simon C.   60
Rouse, Miles Coleman   114
Roy, Louise   213
Ruble, Mandy Elissa   43
Ruby, Robin Carol   63
Russell, Julia   112
Ruvalcaba, Daniel   30
Ryan, Theresa   219
Ryder, Kimberly D.   136
Rydquist, Jason   54

S

Sabo, Rene Michelle   177
Sackett, Tarah Annlouise   72
Saieva, Mariana   237
Salazar, Silvina   59
Salgado, Elsy Alicia   176
Salib, Monalisa   57
Sall, Robert Klaus   25
Sallet, Bonnie F.   206
Sammartino, Theresa Ann   224
Sampson, John K.   97
Sams, Jarrod A.   28
Samuel, Mechelle M.   185
Sanchez, Lupe A.   238
Sanchez, Marco Antonio   162
Sanchez, Omar Fernando   246
Sanders, Lisa Marie   238
Sanderson, Alexander Daniel   104
Sanguinito, Rachel Elizabeth   123
Sansom, Julie   245
Santangelo, Chloé Collette   209
Santiago, Iris E.   185
Sapinsky, M-J S.   62
Sarkar, Subhankar   33
Sarraf, Elie   161
Saville, Caitlin   202
Sawatzky, Maria   236
Sawchenko, Cheryl Alice   153
Sawisky, Christina Jane   94
Sawyer, Denise   179
Sayles, Matt   114
Schaefer, Anne   169
Schall, Manda Celeste   226
Schell, Jenna Layne   181
Schellhorn, Nadezda Pavlovna   33
Schmenk, Lauren Leona   80
Schoch, Christina   29
Schomaker, Kelly   7
Schroder, Theresa Lynn   6
Schubert, Cindy Lea   113
Schultze, Marjorie   54
Schwartz, Aaron   60
Scione, Mark Robert, Jr.   97
Scott, Adam Thomas   165
Scott, Carrie Ann   103
Seager, Jenny   167
Seck, David Anthony   158
Sederlan, Tania L.   102
Segal, Ari Adam   151
Segal, Natalia   151
Sekavec, Twylia J.   113

Self, Laurie Gayle   117
Selisky, Erika C.   147
Semones, Samantha R.   218
Senick, Melissa A.   8
Serak, Pat A.   160
Seymour, Bonnie Lu   29
Seymour, Jamie Nicholas   246
Shank, Kehley R.   33
Shapiro, Erin   44
Sharkey, Karen T.   207
Sharples, Dawn M.   191
Shaw, Wes T.   125
Shea, Jeffrey John   92
Sheffield, Guy Ann   185
Sheffrin, Paul   66
Shelander, Edward Hampton   200
Sheldon, Victoria J.   121
Shellhorn, Lina Campos   60
Shellnut, Amanda Elsie   26
Shepke, Terri Lynn   31
Sherrell, Teri   231
Shifley, Anne Marie   39
Shortt, Caleb J.   102
Shull, Michael Todd   90
Shults, Angie Marie   105
Shunk, Lori G.   233
Siczkar, Holly Ruth   87
Siebert, Maxim Denis   79
Siedsma, Sarah Ann   101
Silbereisen, Kane Matthew   203
Simmering, Andrew Leroy   55
Sipiora, Danny   109
Skeldon, Brad T. D.   14
Skidmore, Deana   77
Smit, Elizabeth Benita   36
Smith, Brandi Lei   216
Smith, Douglas L.   174
Smith, Gareth   138
Smith, Kelsey M.   175
Smith, Ken   68
Smith, Maxine Masterfield   129
Smith, Sue   247
Snavely, Tyler Joe   167
Snelbaker, Crystal L.   75
Snow, David Gordon   228
Snow, Dezerae Dawn   243
Snyder, Adrienne Florence   231
Somers, Paul A.   159
Sommerfield, Sandra Lee   98
Sonera, Dee   216
Sopczak, Nicholas Adam   127
Sorensen, Jackie Joyce   244
Soucy, Francisco   97
Sousa, Priscilla Patricia   160
Souther, Janet Lynn   211
Sowells, Deletha   89
Spears, Jennifer S.   215
Spencer, Bruce A.   224
Spencer, Natalie Anne   219
Spradling, Carla LeAnn   79
Springer, Meghan   181
Stacy, Andrew Louis   30
Stafford, Morgana Maxine   119
Steciuk, Jordy Raye   117
Steed, Jenetta J.   175
Steele, Samuel Lin   127
Stein, Lauren Elizabeth   2
Steinmetz, Celsie I.   143
Steinmetz, Kelsey Marie   209
Stephany, Mark Dominic   124
Stergiou, Maria   48
Stetter, Joanne   177
Stevens, Sherry Jo   55

Steward, Christopher Morgan   16
Stewart, Denise Ann   121
Stewart, Eric Wayne   228
Stewart, Jennifer   101
Stewart, Josie Cougar   170
Stewart, Katie Elizabeth   110
Stewart, Kristen R.   230
Stewart, Kyle Troy   30
Stidham, Pamela D.   172
Stidman, Alice Marie   144
Stockwell, Heather   2
Stokes, Max D.   242
Stolworthy, Lloyd   10
Stone, Rachael Nicole   221
Stork, Dan James   170
Stout, Martha M.   28
Stratton, Urszula Barbara   110
Straughan, Jennie Theresa   92
Strawser, Linda   199
Streitberger, Marcia Kay   1
Strickland, Janet A.   189
Strobel, Dawn   220
Studd, Terry Charles   76
Studebaker, Audra Marie   209
Studley, Lauren K.   83
Stunkel, Laura Kay   48
Stuver, Karolyn W.   59
Sukert, Michelle   172
Sullivan, Conrad Charels John   133
Sullivan, Stephanie Anne   247
Sultemeier, Leslie Lynn   57
Susong, Parker D.   242
Sutherland, Tara Lyn   195
Swafford, Frederick   178
Swallow, Meg Elizabeth   176
Swarts, John P.   140
Swieboda, Maciej   115
Sylva, Bridget Ann   215
Szymanski, Donald   125

T

Tabaracci, Victoria   135
Takamaa, Mikael Matias   84
Tangel, Kristin Claire   195
Tapia, Sylvana   129
Tarala, Kelly James   62
Tardif, Daniel   95
Tate, Kimberly Ann   118
Tateossian, Keely   244
Taylor, Becky   132
Taylor, Carla Mae   141
Taylor, Drew   4
Taylor, Emma Marshane   42
Taylor, Jacqueline O'shea   222
Taylor, Justin   132
Taylor, Nona Jean   190
Taylor, Samuel Christopher   202
Taylor, Sarah Dolly Minnie   92
Teaff, Jessi Lyn   45
Teague, Christina Michelle   233
Tedford, Taylor   6
Tennisco, Hilda Bernadine   67
Terrana, Rachel Elizabeth   224
Terrill, Tracy Marie   225
Terry, Misty Dawn   23
Teufel, Debbie Alice   102
Teynor, Bonny P.   188
Thill, Rodney Howard   150
Thom, Susan Joy   202
Thomas, Barbara   15
Thomas, Lashondra   160

Thomas, Shay   190
Thompson, Rachel Ze   38
Thompson, Ronette B.   103
Thompson, Stacey   171
Thompson, Susie   185
Tieman, Lewis, Jr.   51
Tipton, Rachel   157
Toborowsky, Linda   73
Todd, Savannah Victoria   211
Tompkins, Felicia Lynn   160
Tompkins, James Edward   33
Towe, Robin L.   184
Tradonsky, Ali Nicole   20
Treaster, Martin John Robert   202
Tremblay, Danielle   207
Trepanier, Keith Andrew   43
Trombino, John Joseph   200
Trueman, Jenn K.   97
Tumiel-Kozak, Eva R.   230
Tungilik, Tanya   57
Turck, Chris Thomas   146
Turek, Karolina Katarzyna   95
Turnbull, Lindsay Rae   179
Tyler, Brandon Maurice   27
Tyler, Julie Beasley   74
Tyo, Joanne Louise   170
Tyrrell, Adam Michael   11
Tyson, Kyle Patrick   40

U

Udall, Josh James   203
Uhl, Marty   226
Underwood, David Edward   239
Underwood, Summer Mae   43
Usherwood, Holly Ann   23
Uskuraiti, Amanda   169
Utter, Corissa Michelle   242

V

Valtierra, Jean   204
Van Arkel, Sara Louise   146
Van Boxmeer, Diane N.   166
Van Herk, Tera Marie   153
Van Leishout, Karl E.   40
Van Zyl, Dean Andrew   31
Van, Lisa M.   184
Vandellen, Jody Lynn   212
Vandenburg, Kirsty   53
Vandeusen, Carole C.   175
Vasquez, Kristine Marie   126
Vasquez, Ricardo   212
Vassallo, Tara Savina   147
Vaughn, Stacey Leana   235
Veguilla, Eduardo   73
Veldhuizen, Heidi Nicole   42
Venkataramana, Anita B.   210
Veroline, Cindy Lynn   95
Versnel, John Cornelius, IV   156
Villeneuve, Colleen Joyce   40
Visintine, Denise Evans   9
Visocsky, Andrea Lynn   87
Vivianiová, Valentina   210
Volk, Courtney M.   161
Von Flatern, Jenny Ellen   74
Vondervoort, Ashley C.   110
Vongphouthone, Siengthong   13

W

Wade, Jason Edward Horace   36
Wagner, Kelsey A.   117
Wait, Joshua J. C.   24
Waite, Gloria Jean   122
Waite, Mary Ann   67
Waldman, Ariel Elizabeth   130
Walker, Benjamin Parks   21
Walker, Cheryl   72
Walker, Megan Renae   221
Walker, Nikki Lynn   92
Walker, Stacey   136
Wallace, Josephine   15
Wallace, Maggie Mae   46
Walsh, Tommy Burton   95
Walther, Traci R.   11
Walton, Lucy Anna   204
Ward, Chris   199
Ward, David Layne   66
Ward, Deanna Lynn   52
Ward, Thomas   41
Warren, David A.   194
Wasim, Haider Quazi   92
Wasiuk, Emily   91
Watson, Christina Love   239
Watson, Jessica Alice   31
Watson, Michelle Renea   216
Webber, Brittany   169
Weber, Kurt R.   213
Weber, Tanya   75
Weckstein, Ariana DeNevi   21
Weigel, Beth   245
Weinisch, Phil   70
Welch, Charlotte   172
Welch, Sandra Lee   73
Weleschuk, Aaron Micheal   112
Wells, Sandy Allyne   67
Wells, Sharon   27
Wengrovius, Zach Elliott   115
Werther, Matthew Allen   45
Wesley, Kayla Dawn   212
West, Herbert D.   231
West, Samantha Vivian   204
Westcott, Kaylee R.   131
Wettstein, Natan   245
White, Carole Elizabeth   201
White, Corey Thomas   8
White, Margaret L.   6
White, Rebekka Lea   57
White, Samantha Janay   24
White, William George   209
Whiteley, Diana L.   84
Whitlow, Francie   49
Whittemore, Ali Elizabeth   134
Whorton, Rebecca   85
Whorton, Sara Elizabeth   123
Wiens, Michaela J.   64
Wiley, Heather Hobbs   194
Wilkie, Gary W.   71
Wilkinson, Deborah   219
Willging, Alexandria Jo   163
Williams, April Renee   128
Williams, Cheryl Hodges   165
Williams, Debra   123
Williams, Demetrius M.   223
Williams, Misty   153
Williamson, Josh Bentley   6
Wilson, David W.   213
Wilson, Tracey Lynnette   158
Wilson, Whitney Rae   165
Winkler, Brandy Marie   175

Winns, Brandon Michael   4
Winslow, Sam Burke   243
Winters, Joe   239
Wisner, Nick   8
Witherow, Jenna Rae   191
Wolf, Sara Katherine   233
Wood, Brigit   111
Wood, Kimberly Ann   192
Wood, Seileen P.   87
Woodard, Aaron Christmas   20
Woodley-Cardy, Carolyne M.   111
Woodyard, Patty A.   201
Wray, Dillon James   244
Wright, Karen F.   185
Wright, Robert Steve   20
Wrixon, Crystal Alvina-Lee   205

Y

Yakowicz, Patricia Ann   158
Yankey, Deloris   128
Yankey, Rhonda Patrice   180
Yant, Kathie   186
Ybarra, Melinda Sue   61
Yeoman, Bobby Jean   165
Yocke, Dave M.   82
Yoon, Ji-yun Yuna   114
Yopp, Terry   101
Young, Angelia M.   24
Young, April G. I. M.   80
Young, Erin Rebecca Ward   3
Young, Mrs. Colby R.   166
Young, Nancy Emery   39
Young, Traci Lynn   7

Z

Zabron, Aga J.   168
Zanzig, Jennifer Lynn   198
Zavada, Carissa   115
Ze-Dukes, Carlos Ezekiel   37
Zeller, Tessa Ann   23
Zhecheva, Liana Ivaylova   233
Ziebell, Rhiannon Jane   173
Zuesi-Kreu, Maribeth   71